I HELD LINCOLN

T0327040

I Held Lincoln

A Union Sailor's Journey Home

RICHARD E. QUEST

Potomac Books

AN IMPRINT OF THE UNIVERSITY OF NEBRASKA PRESS

Unless otherwise indicated, the illustrations in the gallery
are used courtesy of Mr. and Mrs. John Loring Hamm.

Manufactured in the United States of America.

Library of Congress Cataloging-in-Publication Data
Names: Quest, Richard E., author.
Title: I held Lincoln: a union sailor's journey home /
Richard E. Quest.
Description: Lincoln: Potomac Books, an imprint of the
University of Nebraska Press, 2018.
Identifiers: LCCN 2017044998
ISBN 9781612349497 (cloth: alk. paper)
ISBN 9781640120549 (epub)
ISBN 9781640120556 (mobi)
ISBN 9781640120563 (pdf)
Subjects: LCSH: Loring, Benjamin, 1824–1902. | United
States—History—Civil War, 1861–1865—Prisoners and
prisons. | Prisoners of war—United States—Biography.
| Prisoners of war—Confederate States of America—
Biography. | Escaped prisoners of war—United States—
Biography. | Ship captains—United States—Biography. |
United States. Navy—Officers—Biography. | Louisiana—
History—Civil War, 1861–1865—Campaigns. | Calcasieu
River (La.)—History, Military—19th century. | Lincoln,
Abraham, 1809–1865—Assassination.
Classification: LCC E611 .Q47 2018 | DDC 973.7/7092 [B]—
dc23 LC record available at https://lccn.loc.gov/2017044998

Set in New Baskerville ITC Pro by Mikala R Kolander.

In Memory
Of the martyred prisoners who wore the blue
And died that the Nation might live;
Of the War-worn Veterans
Who survive to reap the benefit
And share the glory of the living Nation.

—Loring's personal log, 1864

CONTENTS

List of Illustrations ix

Preface: The Loring Project xi

Acknowledgments xv

Author's Note xvii

1. Getting in the Fight 1

2. The *Wave* 6

3. A Seasick *Wave* 9

4. No Coal 13

5. The Enemy Is Close By 17

6. A Precious Rose 20

7. Chicken Feed 22

8. Prison 25

9. Escape! 28

10. Through the Wall 34

11. On the Outside 43

12. Plantations 53

13. Dog Ranch 60

14. De Doe Is Dead?! 65

15. The Hunter 69

16. Interrogation 75

17. A Night Drive 78

18. A Confederate Bastille 81

19. Anderson Grimes County Jail 83

20. The Old Pen Again 89

21. Deadliest Killer 94

22. Making the Best of It 96

23. The Swamp 100

24. Tied Up. 104

25. The Power of the Pen(cil) 109

26. Navigating by the Wind 114

27. Parched Corn 118

28. Over the River and through the Woods . . 122

29. Bear Swamp 124

30. Confederate Potatoes. 128

31. Goodbye, Texas 132

32. Home Guard and Yankee Prisoners 134

33. Old Friends? 138

34. Your Passes or Your Life! 142

35. Where Is My Penknife? 150

36. The Last Toenail 156

37. A Burned Bridge 159

38. Chimneys on the Horizon 163

39. Lincoln Coffee and a Civilized Bed 166

40. The Surprise. 168

41. Washington Navy Yard 170

42. I Held Lincoln 173

Afterword 177

Notes 179

Bibliography 189

ILLUSTRATIONS

Following page 88

1. Gold coins carried by Loring
2. Loring's mustering-in papers
3. Document showing Loring's promotion to lieutenant
4. Loring's orders to command the USS *Wave*
5. Map of the capture of the USS *Wave* and *Granite City* and escape route from Camp Groce
6. Forged pass that Loring used for the second escape
7. Loring's handwritten escape map and notes
8. Map of escape route taken by Loring and Flory from Camp Groce
9–10. Flory and Loring dressed in their Confederate escape clothes
11. Letter acknowledging Loring's escape from Camp Groce
12. Letter placing Loring at the Washington Navy Yard two days before the Lincoln assassination
13–14. Loring's penknife, given to him by his sister Lillie
15. Loring's navy frock coat worn at Ford's Theatre
16. Loring's grave in Evergreen Cemetery, Owego, New York
17. A postwar portrait of Loring

PREFACE

The Loring Project

My parents can attest to the fact that I have always been interested in history and things that were old. Growing up in a "historic" house in upstate New York contributed to that interest as I explored the various nooks and crannies of that old house as a child. Many of our family vacations were spent camping on the East Coast, visiting historic places. One of those vacations took place at Gettysburg, Pennsylvania, with our little camper perched on a small knoll. It would forever change how I viewed history and would solidify my lifelong interest in the Civil War. However, this specific story for me begins in the early 1990s.

As a young high school history teacher I was tasked with teaching U.S. history to eleventh-grade students. It became very apparent very quickly that I had to do something unique not only to garner my students' attention but to keep it throughout the year. Otherwise why should they be interested in history that always seemed to happen to someone else, somewhere else? I started doing my own research into local history to make my classes more relevant. Research trips to local libraries, historical societies, and museums provided enough information for me to begin to infuse local history into the New York State Regents' curriculum. I found that as I did so students became more interested and engaged and participated more often during class. The material, it seemed, had become more relevant to the students. This would later become the topic of my doctoral dissertation at the University of Pennsylvania.

In 1993 I was introduced to Emma Sedore, at that time the Town of Owego historian, and Jean Neff, the executive director of the Tioga County Historical Society. I explained to them that I was a teacher and was interested in local Civil War history that I could work into my lesson plans. Emma told me the story of a Union sailor who had lived in Owego after the Civil War, had attended Ford's Theatre, and had come in contact with President Lincoln the night of the assassination. She mentioned that this veteran's frock coat was part of the collection in the Tioga County Historical Society. This prompted me to visit the historical society and meet with Jean Neff, who told me a similar story, showed me Lt. Benjamin W. Loring's frock coat, and mentioned that it had President Lincoln's blood on it. I was intrigued.

In 1994 I was appointed the Tioga County historian, a position I held until I resigned in 2001. (As the seventh county historian, I thought it appropriate to serve for seven years). During this time I had access to many historical records and archives, in which I was able to conduct research in order to create lesson plans ranging in time from the Revolutionary War through World War II. Later this would evolve into the creation of an entire elective course for students and adults as well.

The story of Lieutenant Loring was always one that students seemed particularly interested in while we studied the Civil War, and so I began to delve deeper. In the fall of 1998 I began to research Loring's frock coat specifically. In the spring of 1999 Emma Sedore made arrangements to introduce me to Mr. and Mrs. John Loring Hamm, John being Lieutenant Loring's great-grandson. We met at the Tioga County Historical Society and John shared with me one of his family's treasured heirlooms. It was a small penknife inscribed on one side with the date, "April 14th, 1865 B.W. Loring Lieut. USN," and on the other side with "This knife cut the Tie from the neck of President Lincoln when assassinated." That was it. As soon as I saw this I knew I had to learn more and provide irrefutable evidence that Loring had indeed assisted President Lincoln. I was determined to forensically prove this and thus began my search for President Lincoln's DNA.

I next considered identifying the blood on Loring's frock coat, taking a sample, having DNA analysis done, and then comparing it to a known Lincoln DNA sample to forensically prove that Loring had come in contact with Lincoln. Easier said than done. It would take years to attempt this, and with no budget I relied on the interest and generosity of others. During this time I worked with the board of directors at the Tioga County Historical Society, scientists and geneticists at Reliagene Labs and Lakehead University, and a conservator at the Rochester Museum and Science Center. I acquired Lincoln hair samples with excellent provenance and, along with blood samples taken from the frock coat with the permission of the Tioga County Historical Society, I was able to retrieve partial DNA results from the hair samples, which have never been publicized. This took years to complete.

Finally, in March 2014 it was clear to me that it was time to tell Loring's story. I looked through my notes from the previous fifteen years and made a phone call that would change everything. I called John Loring Hamm. I wasn't sure if the phone number was still good, if he would remember me, or if he would even be open to a discussion. John answered the phone. I told him who I was and asked if he remembered me from many years ago. He said he certainly did. I was nearly at a loss for words. I explained that I wanted to write a book about his ancestor Lieutenant Loring and wondered if we could talk further about it. He explained that he and his wife, Terri, were about to retire and needed to focus on the transition at work and home. He promised he would get back in touch with me after they retired and we could discuss it further. I was excited.

John is a man of his word, just like his great-grandfather. As promised, John called in May, we discussed the project, and John and Terri invited me and my wife, Patti, to visit them to see what material they had that might be relevant to the story. John, Terri, and their entire family, past and present, have done an outstanding job of protecting and preserving family documents and artifacts. Those materials and the family's oral history have been the foundation for this book. The book is the culmination of nearly twenty years of research, three years of writing, and a phone call made fifteen years after an initial introduction, which has led to an enduring friendship. All of this owes its genesis to a patriotic Union sailor resolved to report for duty and get in the fight, his great-grandson's passion for preserving family history, and a young teacher's efforts to find a way to make history more interesting, engaging, and relevant for his students.

ACKNOWLEDGMENTS

First and foremost I would like to acknowledge Mr. and Mrs. John Loring Hamm, without whom this book would have never been possible. Thank you for sharing your family's history, for providing unfettered access to a seemingly endless archive of documents, for enduring countless phone calls to clarify information and ask additional questions, and for trusting me to get it right. Thank you for your friendship and for the privilege and honor to tell Lt. Benjamin W. Loring's story. It is my sincere hope that John's great-grandfather, Lieutenant Loring, would approve.

I would like to thank Emma Sedore, the former Town of Owego historian and current Tioga County historian, my successor in that position, for making me aware of the legend of the "Civil War Coat" and for introducing me to Mr. and Mrs. John Loring Hamm so many years ago. Thank you to Jean Neff, former executive director; Joann Lindstrom and Pam Goddard, former codirectors; and Staci Becker, current executive director of the Tioga County Historical Society. Thank you to the board of directors, staff, and volunteers of that organization, both past and present, for their help and support during my research and for providing access to the Loring frock coat and related artifacts. A warm thank you to the Candor Central School District for supporting my research efforts in and out of the classroom. A special thank you to Dr. Jonathan Zisk, my colleague and friend from Candor High School, for his help and support during the early phases of this research. My deepest appreciation to Dr. Sudhir Sinha and Gina Murphy from Reliagene Labs and to Stephen Fratpietro from the Paleo DNA lab at Lakehead University for their scientific expertise and generosity in support of my early research. A warm thank you to Ralph Wiegandt, formerly of the Rochester Museum and Science Center and now with the National Science Foundation in collaboration with the University of Rochester, for his conservation efforts and sampling expertise. Thank you to John Reznikoff from the University Archives for the very generous donation of Lincoln material. Thank you to Danial Francis Lisarelli for sharing his in-depth knowledge of Camp Groce prison near Hempstead, Texas, and for his efforts in preserving the memory of those who never left that prison. Many thanks to Robert Krick Jr., chief historian at Richmond National Battlefield Park, for his expertise and time touring the battlefield at Drewry's Bluff. A very special thank you to Webster Stone, my initial editor, who early on recognized the merits of this story and understood my resolve and passion to bring this to publication. Your guidance, mentoring, and support of my writing were instrumental in the development of this book and its publication. A tremendous thank you to Tom Swanson and the University of Nebraska Press team for agreeing to bring Lieutenant Loring's amazing story to print. The team's support in all aspects and phases of the publishing process has been an incredible experience.

Thank you to my parents for those wonderful childhood vacations that would fuel my passion for history and for indulging my searching, digging, and rummaging around, including under the floorboards of my childhood home. I would like to thank my wife, Patti, for all of her support and love over many years of trying to bring this story to life. She always supported my efforts and knows better than anyone how important this has been to me. Thank you to my children, Crystal and Rick, for enduring too many family vacations to nearly every East Coast Civil War battlefield or museum related to my research.

Finally, I would like to thank Lt. Benjamin W. Loring for heeding the call of his country to report for duty with steadfast resolve and grit to help free those in bondage. For his dedication to the men he served with, for his self-sacrifice, and for leaving behind his thoughts and words that were witness to this crucible of American history so that they might echo through time.

AUTHOR'S NOTE

This story is based on actual historical events from 1861 to 1866, derived from official U.S. government documents, official U.S. Navy orders, and the personal log, letters, journals, notes, and oral family history of Lt. Benjamin W. Loring, USN. Quotations taken directly from Loring's personal log are cited in the notes. Other conversations throughout the book are representations based on documents, letters, and oral family history, designed to help tell the story. All names of participants and places in the story are those of real people and places.

I HELD LINCOLN

Getting in the Fight

The monitor USS *Weehawken* had run aground a mere twelve hundred yards from Fort Moultrie in Charleston Harbor, South Carolina, and was taking heavy fire from the Confederate batteries inside the fort.[1] Union naval lieutenant Benjamin W. Loring yelled to his gun crew, "Fire!" The *Weehawken's* 15-inch Dahlgren gun belched and sent a 330-pound shell screaming toward Fort Moultrie. Loring's calm demeanor reassured his men. Only a few weeks earlier he had sighted and fired the first Union shell at Fort Sumter since it had been lost to the Confederates two years previously. It was deadly business, but he knew he had to be in the fight. "Reload!" As Loring's men worked to reload the massive gun his mind wandered back to more peaceful times for the briefest of moments.

On the side of a steep trail in the Sierra Nevadas of California Ben Loring knelt next to a small fire and warmed his hands. He reached for a steaming pot of coffee, filled a tin cup, and handed it to his younger brother, Bailey, before topping off his own. It was the middle of November 1861 and it was very cold. Loring unfolded the Monday, November 18, edition of the *Sacramento Union* and perused the columns. The first story that jumped out at him described another Union defeat at a place called Ball's Bluff in Virginia. Nearly one thousand soldiers had been killed or wounded during the battle. U.S. Senator Edward Baker, a colonel with the Federal forces at Ball's Bluff and a personal friend of President Lincoln, had been killed during the battle.[2] Loring let that sink in for a moment and then slapped the paper against his thigh. Startled, Bailey jumped, spilling half his coffee. Glaring at his brother, he wondered what had gotten into him. No longer able to contain himself, Loring expressed his frustration through clenched teeth and tight lips. He explained to Bailey that he was sure the secessionists were going to tear the country apart. Loring had been agitated ever since the Confederates had fired on Fort Sumter in April

1861. Loring stood up, showed the newspaper to Bailey, and then read the story again himself. The words stared back at him in black and white. It was crystal clear: this was not just a disagreement that could be settled by disorganized troops brawling, as they had in the debacle at Bull Run. This was war. Loring looked his younger brother and business partner in the eye. In a low, calm, resolved voice he stated, "Bailey, I need to get in the fight. It is time. I must report, it is my duty." Loring wadded the paper up and threw it on the fire, muttering to himself, "Not on my watch." He was not going to allow these rebellious Southerners to tear his country apart even if it meant he had to lay down his life to prevent it.

Bailey turned away. He knew there was no point in arguing with his brother. He tightened the packs on the string of mules as Loring kicked snow on the fire, extinguishing it. The brothers made their way up the trail on their final trip together to deliver supplies to the gold miners in the mountains. After returning to Sacramento in the middle of January, Loring turned the entire business over to Bailey.

With only the clothes on his back, a few small personal items stuffed into a carpetbag, and a handful of gold coins tucked into his waist belt, Loring boarded a mail coach heading east. Riding on top of the mail bags, Loring bounced across the vast, wild continent for twelve days.[3] Reaching Washington DC and the Navy Yard, he wasted no time and was mustered into service in the U.S. Navy on February 6, 1862. Commissioned an officer with the rank of acting master, he was ordered to report to Cmdr. A. Taylor in Mystic, Connecticut.[4]

Just ninety days later, Loring found himself on the James River at Drewry's Bluff on board the USS *Galena* in command of a guns division as part of Gen. George B. McClellan's Peninsular Campaign.[5] A year later, in June 1863, Loring and the crew of the USS *Weehawken* captured the Confederate ironclad ram *Atlanta*. Loring had the honor of commanding the *Atlanta* and guiding it into harbor. Just five months later he would do the same with the captured British schooner and blockade runner *Alma*, delivering the ship and its British captain, George Gordon, to naval authorities in Charleston harbor.[6] Those were heady days. For his "gallant conduct in action" Loring was promoted to lieutenant on July 13, 1863.[7]

Getting in the Fight

At the request of Capt. John Rodgers, he was transferred to and given command of the guns division and made the executive officer (second in command) on board the ironclad monitor USS *Weehawken*. The *Weehawken* was a formidable ship of the line. Crewed by seventy-five men, it was two hundred feet long with five inches of iron protecting its hull. Eleven inches of iron surrounded the turret, which accommodated imposing 15-inch and 11-inch Dahlgren guns.

Loring snapped back to attention as the turret pivoted about, bringing the bore of the 15-inch gun to point at its next target. He sighted down the barrel until Fort Moultrie was squarely in its sights, just across Charleston Harbor from Fort Sumter. Satisfied with the alignment, he again gave the order to fire. Flames burst from the maw of the big gun and the shell arced toward the fort. The huge Union shell found its mark. It hit an 8-inch Columbiad, splitting its barrel.[8] Fragments of the shell and canon sheared off, throwing deadly shrapnel inside the fort. Metal chunks tore through nearby ammunition chests, igniting them. A horrific explosion erupted. Those men who were unlucky enough to be standing close by were ripped apart. Wood, stone, dirt, and pieces of men were flung one hundred feet into the air. Loring could see the explosion before the sound reached him and his men. He again gave the order "Reload!"

Loring put his hand in his pocket. He felt the ever-present pen-knife his sister Lillie had given him as a keepsake. He smiled to himself. He recalled making the trip by steamer around Cape Cod to Duxbury, Massachusetts, in February 1862 to visit his family while on leave from duty in Connecticut. He remembered Lillie's parting words as they said goodbye and she kissed him on the cheek. "I hope this will be of some use to you. Think of me as you use it." It had been a tender moment. It was all dangerous business now. Loring and his crew had caused many deaths, but he reminded himself that it was they, the rebels, who had started this conflagration.

The Confederate artillery was slow to recover from the hit on the Columbiad, but its reply soon quickened. Loring was knocked off his feet. The concussion was so loud he didn't actually hear it but instead felt it. It was as if the entire ship was going to cave in upon him. Quickly regaining his feet, he looked at his stunned men as they got back to work. He reassured the men, reminding them that the Confederate shells couldn't penetrate eleven inches of iron at this distance. With the gun reloaded, Loring sighted down the 13-foot barrel. Those Rebs knew there was hell to pay. "Fire!" Acrid smoke from thirty-five pounds of powder belching out of the muzzle filtered back into the turret, half blinding and choking the men. "Reload!"

Loring's mind again wandered. He recalled his days at sea as a young man, sailing around the world as a mere deckhand. He had been taught how to sail, tie the obligatory knots, and navigate by the stars by some of the saltiest sailors the sea had to offer. He recalled his youthful exuberance and eagerness to climb the ranks until he had finally been awarded a captaincy of his own. Yes, indeed, those were simpler days. But Loring was determined to do his duty to help put down this rebellion so he and the rest of the country could return to more peaceful times.

Loring again focused his attention. "Fire!" The 15-inch smooth-bore again spoke with authority and sent another shell toward Fort Moultrie. Another incoming shell hit the *Weehawken*'s turret. The concussion threw the men to the floor. Loring caught himself and again reassured his men. The men could feel the massive propeller straining to pull the ship off the bar. With a shudder the ship lurched forward and began to pull free. The 15-inch Dahlgren gun barked and sent a parting shot toward the pile of rubble that used to be Fort Moultrie as the *Weehawken* steamed back to port and safety. It would be up to the army now to send in troops to take the fort.

That evening Loring made his official report to Captain Rodgers. Rodgers, glad to have escaped the fray, commended Loring for his keen work with the Dahlgren guns and his calm demeanor under fire. In his official report of the event, Captain Rodgers recommended Loring for command of his own ship. This was brought to the attention of Rear Admiral Dahlgren himself and was acknowledged by the secretary of the navy, Gideon Welles, on October 21, 1863.[9] Not long afterward Loring was ordered to report to Washington.

Upon his arrival in Washington Loring met with the assistant secretary of the navy, Gustavus V. Fox. Fox explained to Loring that the recently promoted Commodore Rodgers had requested Loring to serve with him aboard the double-turreted monitor USS *Dictator*, currently under construction. Fox further explained that the ship would not be completed for some time and that he would either put Loring on waiting orders until it was finished or provide Loring with temporary duty; the decision was Loring's. Eager to fulfill his duty and stay in the fight, Loring accepted the temporary orders and was transferred to the Mississippi Squadron.

The *Wave*

November 13, 1863, dawned brisk and breezy. Loring leaned into the wind as he walked the quarter mile from the spare room he was renting to the Navy Yards in Washington. As he entered the headquarters office a clerk handed him an envelope.[1] His orders from Rear Adm. David Porter, commander of the Mississippi Squadron, had come through. Loring was detached from the USS *Clara Dolsen* and ordered to report to Acting Ensign C. W. Litherbury and to seek out Joseph Brown, a contractor in Cincinnati, Ohio, and take command of the newly retrofitted USS *Carrabassett*.[2] Loring was to oversee the final details of the retrofitting, then take that ship downriver to Cairo, Illinois, at the junction of the Ohio and Mississippi Rivers, and finally report with the ship to New Orleans. Loring stopped at the paymaster's office, collected his $39.60 in mileage for the trip, and made overland arrangements to travel the 396 miles from Washington to Cincinnati.[3] Five days later he reported to Fleet Capt. A. M. Pennock, commanding the naval station in Cairo, and took command of the *Carrabasset*. Once the retrofitting was completed he guided the ship down the Ohio to the Mississippi and to New Orleans. On March 22 Loring steamed into New Orleans aboard the *Carrabasset*, where he immediately received orders. He was detached from the *Carrabasset* and ordered to take command of the retrofitting of the USS *Wave*.[4] Finally Loring was at the seat of war in the Mississippi Squadron. He was anxious to complete the work on the *Wave* and get in the fight.

The USS *Wave* was built on the Monongahela River just south of Pittsburgh and had been completed in 1863. Originally christened the *Argosy II*, it was renamed the USS *Wave*, as there was already a ship named *Argosy* and having two was not only confusing but considered unlucky. A stern-wheeled transport with a shallow draught, it was designed to haul cotton and cattle on the rivers, not fight a rebellion.

Loring had his work cut out for him. He needed to make sure that the ship was properly outfitted for combat, and he needed to recruit a crew. He had never shied away from a challenge, but this would prove to be one of the greatest he had ever faced. Loring had served on several ships, including the USS *Galena*, an ironclad ship of war, and the USS *Weehawken*, a single-turreted monitor with cutting-edge technology and weaponry. Now his first combat command would be that of a retrofitted barge formerly used for the transport of cotton.

Loring stood at the dock in New Orleans, his hands on his hips, and thought to himself that it was "a fearful fall! From ironclad to an aquatic tinclad wheelbarrow."[5] Regardless, Loring was determined to do his duty and get into the fight. One of the shipwrights pointed at Loring as he stared at the ship. The other men stopped and turned around. It was clear that this man in the navy uniform was in command. Loring walked up the gangplank, and as he boarded the *Wave* he smiled. He could feel it, the ship belonged to him.

It was a tall ship, which was impressive, but a large amount of upper works would have a habit of catching the wind. It also had a shallow draught, only four and a half feet. This was ideally suited for the rivers, but in deep-blue waters in any kind of a crosswind this would potentially cause it to become unwieldy and difficult to handle. Loring walked about on the main deck admiring the ship. As he leaned over the port side he saw a dozen faces looking up at him. He had clearly interrupted the work crews. Loring commented to no one in particular that it looked like the ship "could run in a heavy dew."[6] A few heads nodded. Loring's brow furrowed as he strode quickly back down the gangplank. There was still much work to do.

Loring needed a crew now that the work retrofitting the *Wave* was well under way. He located the recruiting office in New Orleans and began the task of recruiting men. The officers would be assigned, of course, but it was up to Loring to recruit sixteen seamen, for a total crew of fifty-nine.[7] After some discussion with naval authorities in New Orleans Loring was pleased to receive Ensign Franklin J. Latham as his executive officer, along with Ensigns Peter

Howard and William Millen. Ensign Howard in particular had seen extensive action, and word had spread of his heroism as a boatswain's mate on the USS *Mississippi*.[8] Loring had heard that Congress was going to recognize Howard with a newly created medal, given for extreme heroism, and he was glad to have such a leader onboard the *Wave*. Loring also sought out experienced men to run the mechanicals of the ship and was assigned John Thomson, Michael Rogers, and Michael Fitzpatrick as his engineers.[9]

Loring and his officers quickly found that recruiting men with actual naval experience was nearly impossible. Most of the men and those few boys living in the area were river rats. What sailing experience they had was gained aboard small sailing ships and boats transporting livestock, cotton, and other goods up and down the rivers that spilled into the Gulf Coast. With some patriotic persuasion Loring cobbled together a crew of fifty-nine to man the *Wave*. The crew consisted of "all shades of color from sooty-black to creamy-white, and all ages and conditions of men and boys." However, only a handful of the enlisted men had ever actually been to sea. On April 15 Loring and Ensign Latham strolled about the deck of the *Wave*, inspecting the 156-foot-long, 219-ton ship. Armed with four howitzers broadside, one smoothbore, and one converted rifle in the bow casement, it was ready for action.[10]

Loring received his orders to head down the Gulf Coast to Calcasieu Pass, Louisiana. It was a journey that would force the converted freshwater man o' war to cross the Gulf of Mexico. He knew this would be a dangerous trip for a ship with such a shallow draught and keel. But he would follow orders to the best of his ability. Loring gave orders to cast off the bow and stern lines. With a full head of steam in the boilers, the great paddle wheel at the stern of the ship dug into the muddy waters of the Mississippi River. Loring nodded and the pilot pointed the bow of the *Wave* toward the briny blue waters of the Gulf of Mexico.

3

A Seasick *Wave*

On April 17, 1864, the *Wave* reached the Gulf of Mexico along with its sister ship the USS *Granite City*. The gulf waters roiled. Rather than run the risk of capsizing on the ship's maiden voyage, Loring decided to wait until the seas settled. The following day the *Wave*'s baptism was completed as it plunged into the salty waters of the Gulf of Mexico and sailed toward the Calcasieu River.

After they had sailed only a short distance a crescendo of retching and heaving emanated from below decks. Most of the crew were doubled over. Their faces were green and their guts in knots. The ship rocked side to side as it rose up on the swells and slammed back down. Sailors grabbed for buckets or raced to the side of the ship and spewed chunks of their morning's salt pork rations, chumming the sea. The crew's seasick initiation into the blue-water naval service was less than dignified.

Late in the day the wind increased and with it so did the swells. The *Wave* began to skim across the water, its shallow keel not designed to handle such torrid conditions. The upper works acted like a sail. The ship was blown several degrees off course and the pilot's corrections to the rudder had minimal effect. The ship began to creak as the swells increased. Out of sight of land, Loring ordered the pilot to make for the nearest harbor to avoid foundering and sinking.

Just after sunset Loring left the wheelhouse to look at the sea charts and determine the nearest safe harbor. Quickly reviewing the charts, he noted that they were dangerously close to several reefs. He rushed back to the deck. In a commanding tone he told the pilot, "We cannot run far on this course without clipping a point."[1] The pilot argued with Loring, stating that he knew the waters well. There was no imminent danger. Loring interrupted the pilot, pointing: "There's a reef now!" Dead ahead was a rocky point. The wind was too strong and prevented the ship from turning in time to avoid disaster. The *Wave* and its crew were going to be pushed up onto the reef and be crushed. Yelling above the wind, Loring ordered both anchors dropped to keep the *Wave* from being destroyed on the rocks. Both anchors peeled out of the capstan and caught, spinning the ship around. Anything not tied down spilled across the deck. Barrels, crates, and men slid about.

The depth was only nine feet and the swells were long. The ship pitched about so badly that at times men at one end of the ship would be looking up or down at the men at the other end. The torque placed on the ship and the anchor chains was tremendous. The *Wave* was never designed to handle such heavy seas. Loring and the crew could hear the ship's timbers grinding and creaking. The men held on to any beam or rope they could find and prayed it would hold together. The chains holding the anchors strained near their limit. Loring ordered the stern wheel to slow ahead to relieve some of the tension. This helped, but occasionally the ship would surge and snap back on the chains. Loring went below decks to reassure the men. A veteran of many battles, he had faced death before. But compared to this storm he would have preferred "the thundering of big guns and the shrieking and bursting of shells."[2] All any of them could do was weather the storm and pray.

Throughout the night the wind howled. The sleepless men wondered if the storm would ever subside. Suddenly the ship jerked forward and it sounded as if a canon had been fired. The ship vibrated at its core and swung around. One of the anchor chains had come apart! The ship drifted perilously close to the rocks and bobbed on the water until the remaining anchor grabbed the sandy bottom. But as the ship reached the top of a swell the anchor would pull loose and the ship would move closer to the rocks and certain destruction. Finally, as the *Wave* came down from a swell, the anchor grabbed the bottom and jerked to a stop, the remaining chain near the point of breaking. All night Loring stayed on watch in the wheelhouse, straining to see through the inky darkness and how close they were to the reef. Only in the early morning light could Loring and the crew see just how close they were to the rocks and certain death.

At midday the wind began to abate. The *Wave*'s stern was only a few rods from the rocks. Loring ordered the crew to use the steam-powered capstan attached to the remaining anchor chain to slowly reel the ship away from the rocks. Simultaneously he ordered the stern wheel to slow ahead. The tension on the capstan was tremendous. As it slowly turned it began to give way. At first they heard just a crack. Then it sounded like a squad of soldiers firing their muskets as the ship's decking and timbers gave way under the pressure. The crew was ordered to rig a block and tackle to hold them. Late in the day the wind died down enough for the *Wave* to pull anchor. With visible cracks in its hull, it was taking on water fifteen miles from the nearest harbor.

Loring, distrustful of the pilot, watched closely from the wheelhouse as the pilot guided them toward land. Early that evening the wind began to build again and the ship started to drift off course. The damaged ship skittered across the tops of the waves and then slowly plunged forward. Headway was minimal. Loring signaled to the uss *Granite City* for help. The *Granite City* threw several lines to the *Wave* and towed it into Atchafalaya Bay.

Safely in harbor, Loring inspected the *Wave*. The midship section was heavily damaged and leaking. The oakum used to seal the seams of the ship had been completely lost due to the grinding of the ship's timbers in the swells, and several planks had been cracked. The ship was no longer seaworthy. Loring sent word to naval personnel at New Orleans that the *Wave* was in need of major repairs, required recoaling to fuel its engines, and was in need of the services of a competent coastal pilot. The *Wave* had used most of its coal battling the storm and was down to its last ton. Under close scrutiny Loring ordered the pilot to take the *Wave* into East Cote Blanche Bay and sail close to the inner side of Marsh Island toward the eastern side of Vermillion Bay, thus avoiding the worst of the wind. The uss *Ella Morse*, carrying dispatches, met Loring and the *Wave*. Loring summarily dismissed the incompetent pilot and asked the commander of the *Ella Morse* for some much-needed coal for the *Wave*'s bunkers. There was none to be had.[3] Loring sent word back to New Orleans via the *Ella Morse* requesting a competent coastal pilot and coal for refueling. The navy acknowledged the recent events and sent Loring a pilot, but there was no coal available.

The crew was happy to be alive, and repairs to the *Wave* were completed ahead of schedule. Cautiously Loring waited for the weather to fully clear before heading back out into the gulf. With little coal left to fuel the boilers, Loring did not have enough fuel to battle the sea and so was towed by the *Ella Morse*. Arriving two days later, the *Wave* anchored off the Mermentau River. The following day the *Granite City* arrived. With heavy guns loaded the ships slowly steamed toward the mouth of the Calcasieu River, trying to conserve coal. Loring and the crew of the *Wave* were eager and ready to engage Confederate forces.

4

No Coal

Loring gave the order for all hands on deck. The gun crews made ready. The *Wave* crept within range of the Confederate fort guarding the entrance to the Calcasieu River as a bead of sweat appeared on Loring's brow. "Fire!" The 24-pound Dahlgren gun barked and sent a shell arcing toward the fort. It was followed by a second round from the starboard-side gun. "Reload. Fire!" Loring watched, waiting for a response from the fort. The crew waited, ready to fully engage and rain death down on the enemy. "Fire!" Two more rounds screamed toward the fort. The smoke from the big guns hugged the water. No response. The fort was abandoned.[1]

Loring motioned to the pilot to move ahead slowly toward the mouth of the river. As Loring leaned over the side of the *Wave* he gauged the distance between the ship and the riverbank. He again motioned to the pilot to guide the ship closer to the port side. The *Wave* barely squeezed through the shallow narrows of the Calcasieu River Pass. The ship's great paddle wheel churned as the *Wave* slowly moved upriver two miles. Arriving at their destination, the *Wave* dropped anchor near Leesburg, Louisiana (present-day Cameron), opposite the river home of Duncan Smith. The crew went about their business securing the ship as Loring made ready to head ashore to meet with Smith.

Loring's orders were to locate Smith, a local Union sympathizer, and make arrangements to take Smith, his family, and other refugees onboard. Many of the refugees had been hiding in the swamps and bayous for weeks in fear of retaliation by nearby Confederate forces for their political bias toward the Union. Loring was also ordered to procure 450 head of cattle that some of the local Jayhawkers were willing to sell to the federal government and transport them all safely back to New Orleans.[2]

Loring purposefully strode up the bank of the Calcasieu River along the path to the Smith home and was greeted by Duncan Smith himself. Loring held out his hand. Smith grasped it, stating, "We could not help but hear your arrival." "It is best to be prepared for any contingency," Loring replied. Smith led the way to the house.

In the course of the next hour Smith explained the situation in detail. The Confederate fort at the mouth of the river had been abandoned just a few days earlier. Loring listened and made a note that it would be of great importance to post pickets in four locations to provide ample warning of any approaching Confederate force. Smith agreed to have his sons lead the pickets since they were familiar with the area. Smith made it very clear that Confederate forces were sure to be aware of the presence of the *Wave* and any other Federal ships on the way. Loring would definitely need to secure the area.

A squad of ten men from the *Wave* led by one of Smith's sons was sent to burn the Mud Bayou Bridge west of the Calcasieu River. As they made their way through the bayou the USS *Granite City* was at anchor three hundred yards down river from the *Wave*. Loring ordered a small contingent of men ashore along with a party from the *Granite City* to scout the area and make it known that any refugees seeking protection could board the ships. Concerned about the loyalty of the local populace, Loring had suspected Confederate informants arrested and held onboard the *Granite City*. Each day Loring met with Smith and planned for the following day's picket duty. Loring's small crew of fifty-nine men relied on the help of the crew of the *Granite City*, Smith's sons, and a few refugees to man the picket lines day and night. Under constant Confederate surveillance, people were afraid to take the chance to move to the ships. After three days only a handful of refugees had made the trek to the river seeking safe passage back to New Orleans.

Tension was high, and Loring was concerned not only about the threat of attack but about securing coal for his boilers. He implored naval authorities in New Orleans, explaining that the *Wave* was in desperate need of recoaling.[3] He sent another dispatch via the *Ella Morse*, which was loaded with a cargo of sheep bound for New Orleans, begging authorities there to send a collier with the much-needed coal and for reinforcements of two hundred men. The *Ella Morse* returned three days later but carried only three tons of coal for the *Wave*, barely enough to fire its boilers.[4] The *Wave* could easily accommodate five times that amount of coal in its bunkers. Always resourceful, Loring sent out scavenging parties to gather driftwood to be used in the boilers. Although it would provide some fuel, the wood did not burn hot enough to make the steam they would need to maneuver in battle.

Loring was deeply concerned. How could he carry out his orders if he didn't even have enough coal to fire his boilers? It was becoming increasingly obvious that this part of Louisiana was pro-Confederacy, as few refugees came forth. Loring was sure there was a fight coming, and he was sure he would need reinforcements to continue to have a presence on the Calcasieu River.

Loring pulled his executive officer, Ensign Latham, aside. The men discussed their situation. They would need to send someone to New Orleans to personally persuade authorities to send a recoaling vessel. Both agreed the best man for the job was the paymaster Charles Grace. Grace was told to report to the wheelhouse, where Loring explained the dire situation.[5] Grace was rowed to the *Ella Morse* with the urgent message from Loring that he would deliver in person in New Orleans.

Loring stood on deck and looked west across the river. He had burned the Mud Bayou Bridge, posted pickets, set up twenty-four-hour watches, and held daily briefings with Duncan Smith. He had done everything possible to prepare for an attack. His boilers, however, were cold. They were full of driftwood with pine-pitch knots, ready to be fired quickly should the enemy engage them. Hopefully his pickets would be able to give him a good warning before that happened. Still, he slept only four or five hours a night, always watching, always alert. It was rumored that Confederate infantry had been sighted only thirty miles away at Sabine Pass, Texas. Orders were issued to take all precautions necessary and to report immediately any enemy movements toward the hapless ship.

Smith increased his efforts and cautiously tried to persuade those sympathetic to the Union cause to join him and his family onboard the *Wave*. But even he, a lifelong resident, was unable to persuade even the bravest to join them. As Loring anxiously waited for a ship to recoal the *Wave*, Smith and his family prayed to be safely delivered to New Orleans.

Lieutenant Colonel Griffin of the Confederacy's Twenty-First Texas Battalion stood at the gates of Fort Griffin, Texas, and stared east. He gave the order to distribute five days' rations to his 350 men and then to fall in. As the sun set on May 4 the crews of the *Wave* and *Granite City* were unaware that Confederate canon supported by infantry had taken up the thirty-mile march toward the Union sailors.[6]

5

The Enemy Is Close By

Loring, coffee in hand, stood on deck of the USS *Wave* and watched the dawn of May 6 light up the sky. Stretching and taking a deep breath, he thought what a fine day it would be. With no warning, artillery shells screamed down on the *Wave*, the *Granite City*, and the *Ella Morse*. Loring turned in the direction of the firing. Men ran to their battle stations. Loring yelled to the engineers to fire the boilers. In just minutes the opening artillery salvo turned into a fiercely contested fight with Confederate forces. The enemy was close by, only three hundred to four hundred yards away from the *Wave* and just opposite the *Granite City*.

Loring gave orders to return fire, but the *Wave*'s gun deck was several feet lower than the riverbank, which thus formed a protective breastwork for the Confederates. The *Wave*'s gun crews attempted to sight their guns on the enemy but their rounds were completely missing the intended targets. Loring ordered the gun crews to aim as low as possible. The majority of the *Wave*'s crew manned the two bow guns.

Loring watched as the *Granite City* came under a withering artillery fire. Heavily engaged, he personally led the gun crews, helping to pass powder and shot. The first shot from the pair of 12-pound bow guns ripped a pivoting bolt right out of the deck. The recoil of the gun was too much for the old cotton transport. The gun recoiled so severely it blew past Loring. It missed amputating his legs by only inches.[1]

Enemy shells thundered down on the *Wave* and the other ships. Confederate infantry closed the distance. Loring ordered the gun crew to man the 24-pound smoothbores and bring them to battery. Loring yelled to his firemen. The boilers were just coming up to steam. The damp driftwood sizzled as it sputtered in the boilers. The firemen desperately coaxed the fire to life. Loring ordered the *Wave* to come about to move downriver. A shell rent the air, tore through the half-inch boilerplate protecting the ship's hull, and hit the boiler. What steam had come up screamed out through the ragged hole in the boiler. The pressure dropped so quickly that the *Wave* never moved. The ship was a sitting duck. Shots ripped through the upper works and riddled the boiler with more holes. A well-placed Confederate shell split the muzzle of one of the 12-pounders mounted on the bow, wounding an officer. Loring watched as, thirty minutes into the engagement, the *Granite City* struck its colors and surrendered.[2] Loring yelled to his men, "Come now, boys, give 'em hell!" The enemy's full attention turned toward the *Wave* as the *Ella Morse* slipped its moorings and slid downriver, away from the action.

Loring continued to help man the howitzers. Between passing rounds to be loaded Loring saw a company of Confederates moving toward a vantage point that would provide them with enfilading fire. Loring ordered canister to be loaded. The canon now sprayed its deadly shotgun-like load. The effect was disastrous to the Confederates, killing and wounding dozens of the rebels. The remaining Confederate infantry were ordered up and concentrated their musket fire on the disabled ship, wounding two more of the *Wave*'s crew manning the guns. For over an hour the *Wave*'s tiny crew held off 350 Confederate infantry.[3]

The *Wave* was unable to maneuver. Ammunition ran short, and the crew available to service the guns shrank as the number of wounded grew. Loring saw that the situation had become hopeless. Smith had been an observer throughout the fight, helping to pass powder where needed. But now, with the rebels so close, he chose to take his life in his own hands. Leaving his family on board, he jumped overboard and swam to the opposite shore.

Loring stared at the carnage that surrounded him. There was no honor in needlessly sacrificing lives. Loring gave the order to cease fire and to throw overboard any and all materiel that might be useful to the enemy. Muskets, revolvers, sabers, boarding pikes, ammunition, all were thrown over the side. The crew damaged the elevation screws for the big guns and spiked the barrels. They smashed the handles to the engine compressors, and the paymaster's safe, with all of its contents still secure, was thrown overboard. Loring ordered the magazine flooded and the *Wave* began to sink. Loring ran to his personal quarters, rifled through his sea chest, took the signal book, and burned it. He thought to himself, "Death by one of the six balls which missed me by a few inches would have been preferable," as he surrendered the ship.[4] The shooting stopped.

Loring surveyed the damage the ship had sustained. The upper decks were completely destroyed. The staterooms were gone. Bedding, glasses, crocks, and woodwork were splintered and broken. There was debris everywhere. Loring counted sixty-two holes through the tinclad plating of the outer hull. Making his way to the main deck, Loring had his officers report their losses. Ten crewmen had been wounded. Miraculously, none of the crew had been killed. The rebels boarded the *Wave*, whooping and yelling as they took prisoners. The rebel leaders did not believe Loring when he was asked how many had been killed. They assumed that the Federals threw the dead overboard. With the lack of evidence of those killed, Confederate lieutenant colonel Griffin, a former U.S. Army officer and commander of the 350 men from the Sabine Pass garrison, reported, "10 killed and 20 wounded, and 1 gun dismounted, all done by that cussed stern-wheeler which we thought was a transport." All of the crew from the *Wave* and the *Granite City* were captured. As Loring watched the Confederates board the *Wave* he wondered what had happened to the pickets. Why didn't they give a warning about the approaching Confederates? Those few refugees who had been posted on the road that would have been used by the approaching Confederates had either skedaddled at the first sight of the infantry or had not been as sympathetic to the Union as was thought. None of them were heard from again.

6

A Precious Rose

The fighting had been fierce. But it was strange. The people on the other side never quite seemed to be the enemy. Loring and the other prisoners were treated with a level of courtesy and civilized behavior they had not expected. As part of this civilized treatment the prisoners from the *Granite City* and the *Wave* were allowed to keep their personal effects. The officers were allowed not only to keep what was on their person but to have their sea chests accompany them by wagon to their final destination.

The morning after the battle the prisoners were placed in a line and marched off toward prison but were not told where that was. The wounded traveled by wagon. The officers were "temporarily paroled."[1] This meant that Loring did not have to march in line but was free to move back and forth among those captured as he pleased. The march was difficult. The navy prisoners were not used to trudging the required fifteen miles a day. Loring strode up and down the line of march, encouraging his men to keep up and not to fret. But by the end of the day most of the captives were completely played out. The first night the prisoners were halted at the plantation of Mrs. Griffis.

The exhausted men lay down and fell asleep. The morning came quickly. Loring and the other prisoners faced another fifteen-mile march that would test their mettle. The past few days had left the Union navy men in a sour mood. The initial civilities of their captors had worn off, and several of the rebel guards decided to help themselves to some of the personal items that were being hauled along in the wagons.

It was a scorching-hot day. The march nearly welded the prisoners' boots to their feet. Upon reaching the required daily mileage the column was halted. The enlisted men were told to camp where they stood. The officers were quartered with the family of Mrs. Coffin.

Mary A. Coffin was eighty years old and a tried and true supporter of the Union, and she had no qualms about making that known. The Union naval officers were invited to dinner with Mrs. Coffin, where she sympathized with their current situation and misfortune. After dinner Loring inquired about the fate of Duncan Smith. A rebel officer quipped that Smith "had escaped to the bush."[2] As he said this the officer winked at the man next to him, implying that Smith had been captured and shot as a spy. Loring's thoughts turned to Smith's family.

The next morning Loring and his fellow officers prepared for the day's march. As the men left the tidy little house Mrs. Coffin "stood in the doorway and shook the hand of each officer, with a 'good-bye! God Bless You!'"[3] Loring thanked her for her hospitality and generosity. As he turned to leave Mrs. Coffin handed Loring a single yellow rose, for the yellow rose of Texas. Loring took it and looped it through a buttonhole on his vest.

Outside there was a commotion among some of the men. The black sailors who had served in various capacities aboard the *Wave* and *Granite City* were being "distributed among the inhabitants and reduced to a state of slavery."[4] Lieutenant Colonel Griffin himself chose a black man and declared him to be the spoils of war. Loring loudly protested that these men were prisoners of war. He stepped toward one of the guards but was stopped from going any farther by the point of a bayonet. The Union sailor was tied up and led off like a dog on a leash.

The Union prisoners were formed into a line. After marching for several hours the men reached the shores of Sabine Lake. The bedraggled prisoners were loaded aboard a ramshackle old steamer, the *Sun Flower*, and transported up the Neches River to Beaumont. Unsure of their final destination, Loring and the men could only hope that they would arrive soon. The insecurity of the unknown was beginning to weigh heavily on some of the men. Exhausted, sore, and sick, the men awoke the next morning and were loaded aboard a train bound for Houston.

7

Chicken Feed

Loring and his prison compatriots filed off the train in Houston. They were paraded down the main street, which created quite a spectacle for the local inhabitants. Everyone nearby came out to witness the captured Federals marched in grand review. A half mile outside of the city limits the line of march was halted. The prisoners organized themselves into small groups of six to eight men, or a mess, for cooking. The cooking duties were rotated among the members of the mess.

Rations consisted of cornmeal and bacon. The cornmeal was disgusting. It had a consistency similar to chicken feed, with bits of grit and other unidentifiable ingredients mixed in. The bacon was partially rotted. Sitting down to eat, one of Loring's fellow officers and messmates produced a tin of sardines from a pocket inside his vest. A curious Confederate guard spied the tin and moved closer for a better look. Upon seeing the contents he exclaimed, "What are them things you call sardines?" The guard leaned in to inspect the food. "I'll be darned! If they ain't little fishes!"[1] Loring smiled and retorted, "Well, the food here is as bad as the accommodations."

With dinner complete, the men lay down in the sandy Texas soil and attempted to sleep. It was impossible. Every few minutes the men would roll over and scratch. Even the officers, who were provided the luxury of sleeping in a nearby shed, could not escape the tiny torment of the fleas that called the Texas soil home. Seeking relief, Loring climbed up into the rafters of the shed and draped himself across the beams. Unable to sleep, at least he was out of reach of the ravenous insects.

Dawn broke. Loring dropped down from his perch in the rafters and joined his messmates as they breakfasted on the chicken feed and rancid bacon. For four hours the men waited at the Houston and Texas Central Railroad Depot. The ferocious Texas heat beat down upon them as they waited for a train to take them to their final prison destination, Camp Groce. The waiting was laborious. The Confederate guards became restless. Leaving a skeleton force of guards at the station, most went into Houston to take advantage of any opportunities that might present themselves. Unhappy with their circumstances and not having been paid for months, the rebels nearly rioted in town. Saloons were ransacked, groceries were liberated, and a full-on desertion nearly took place. Confederate officers quelled the little uprising, going so far as to find a local band to play patriotic songs such as "The Bonny Blue Flag" to soothe the war-weary men. Loring was disappointed that the row did not turn into a riot. A crowd of townspeople gathered at the station to see for themselves the Yankee prisoners. As the crowd grew so did their discontent with the uninvited guests. Most simply pointed, while some shook their heads and made derogatory remarks about and to the prisoners. Loring overheard two Southern gentlemen deep in conversation state, "You see they came down here to steal our niggers."[2] Loring felt a twinge deep inside, a reminder of what this war was all about.

With the savage beast quieted and the guards back on duty, the train pulled into the station. The Union prisoners were loaded on board flat cars. The train at first moved slowly and then picked up speed. Loring estimated their maximum speed at ten miles an hour. The train rolled through the countryside, passing various plantations and farms. Word about the Union prisoners had spread, and it seemed like the entire local populace had come out to see the train full of prisoners. Hundreds of people lined the tracks to catch a glimpse of the raiders from the north. Women and children waved handkerchiefs and men bowed as the train slowly crept across Texas. Loring and his fellow prisoners returned the waves, which were not intended for them, with bows and waves of their own, much to the chagrin of the onlookers.

Late in the afternoon the train stopped outside of a prison stockade. As the train halted Loring stiffly stood up. He and the other prisoners stepped off the cars and fell into line alongside the tracks. Loring looked to his right at the long line of sailors. To his left he saw a stockade with enormous wooden doors. He wondered . . .

for how many of the men would this be their last moments alive outside those ominous gates of hell? Only in death would some be liberated. Rusty hinges groaned under the weight of the huge wooden doors as they opened. The line moved toward the gate and "with one grand gulp it swallowed men, . . . and baggage" as the men were ordered to march through to Camp Groce.[3]

8

Prison

Fifty miles northwest of Houston and just three miles outside of Hempstead, Loring and his comrades entered Camp Groce with trepidation and angst, not knowing if they would ever leave. Loring immediately focused his attention and began to make mental notes on the structure. The stockade was rectangular in shape, enclosed by fifteen-foot walls. There were a couple of long sheds about one hundred feet in length and a shorter one about thirty feet long. On the east side of the prison the ground was clear and level. On the west side the ground sloped down toward the wall. Built on top of the walls were sentry boxes every one hundred to two hundred feet. Outside the walls in the distance Loring saw a fallow field with grass growing, and it seemed like there was a small brook that ran toward some woods beyond the field.[1]

The men filtered through the gates and stood staring at the stockade. A Confederate sergeant yelled for the men to form ranks. No one moved; the men were in some sort of shock. Loring barked an order and the men snapped to and fell in. Several Confederate officers came forward and took roll call. The men were counted and told that the enlisted men would bunk in the long sheds and officers in the shorter shed. The provost marshal, Captain McDade, stepped forward and addressed the men. He warned them not to attempt to escape and explained that they would be well cared for. McDade gave an order to one of his lieutenants to have the prisoners empty their pockets and turn the contents over for safekeeping.[2]

Surprised by the order, none of the men had time to hide any of their possessions. Loring took a quick mental inventory of what he had in his pockets. The Union prisoners groaned, and a few broke ranks. The rebel guards quickly corrected this behavior with the butts of their muskets. McDade explained that receipts would be provided for the valuables and they would be returned to the owner upon the cessation of hostilities.

Those men who did not comply or were thought not to have emptied their pockets entirely were roughly searched. Many of the Union men tried to discreetly stuff greenbacks in their shoes, socks, and nether regions. The guards were quick to recognize this and stepped in with bayonets at the ready. Loring pulled out his gold pocket watch and $148 in greenbacks. Looking Captain McDade squarely in the eye, he handed them to him and told him, "I'll see those returned; I will not be here forever." McDade assured Loring he would take good care of them. He also boasted that he would provide Loring with small amounts of the money upon written request and, of course, with the approval of the commanding officer of the prison. Taking a chance that as an officer he would not be subjected to a search, Loring did not relinquish the pocketknife his sister Lillie had given him. Nor did he produce any of the gold coins hidden in his waist belt for good luck, which he had carried with him as a reminder of his days in the Sierra Nevadas. He was not searched.

Captain McDade yelled, "Attention!" The Confederate guards stood erect. Loring looked around. A Confederate colonel and captain strutted through the gates followed by a small entourage of heavily armed guards. Loring thought to himself, "Who is this ol' boy, strutting like the cock of the walk?"

The colonel introduced himself: "I am Colonel Gillespie, commanding officer of Camp Groce." Gillespie had been a Methodist minister, lawyer, and editor prior to the war and was appointed commander of the prison by none other than the president of the Confederacy himself, Jefferson Davis.[3] Gillespie pointed and introduced his second in command, Captain Odlum. Odlum was an Irishman and had been a sergeant in the U.S. Army prior to the rebellion. He had seen action earlier in the war in the Confederate infantry and had been captured and spent some rough time in the Point Lookout Prison in Maryland. He was released in a prisoner exchange, promoted to captain, and sent to Camp Groce to help organize and train the men in military matters.[4]

Colonel Gillespie made it very clear that the men were his prisoners and that any attempt at escape would be severely dealt with. Finished, Gillespie turned with a flourish. Captain Odlum followed along with the entourage that marched out of the prison pen. Captain McDade dismissed the men. Loring turned to the officers of the *Wave* and the *Granite City* and simply stated, "See to your men."

9

Escape!

Prison life was nearly intolerable. For two months Loring and been imprisoned behind the fifteen-foot-high walls of Camp Groce. Many of the men imprisoned with him had become ill; some had died. Survival was a daily challenge. The well inside the prison walls had collapsed three days earlier and the only fresh water available had to be drawn from a small stream outside the prison gates. The sinks overflowed when it rained, causing human waste and filth to flood the low-lying areas in the camp.

The stockade walls prevented a breeze from flowing through the prison. For several weeks the prison gates, albeit heavily guarded, had been opened during the day to allow for fresh air to better circulate. It was one of the few luxuries the prisoners had enjoyed. Now the prison gates were closed at all times, preventing the flow of fresh air throughout the camp. The stench of several hundred men within the two-and-a-half-acre pen became putrid. The sale and delivery of outside foodstuffs was ordered stopped. The *Wave*'s assistant surgeon, Boyden, was no longer allowed outside of the prison to search for herbs and other plants, which had provided some medicinal relief to the suffering soldiers and sailors confined within. This was truly hell on earth.

Colonel Gillespie now imposed a ten-foot dead line within the interior of the prison. The line was not marked. At the discretion of the nearest guard posted at the top of the wall, any prisoner stepping too close to the invisible line was to be shot dead.

Escape became a major preoccupation and focus of discussion for Loring and many of the others in Camp Groce. They quickly realized that knowledge of the surrounding countryside would be of crucial importance should the opportunity to actually breach the walls arise.

Fortunately, a document had come into the hands of the prisoners during the march from the Calcasieu River to Camp Groce. A Confederate officer had presented a map of Texas to one of Loring's messmates. A seemingly strange and propitious gift to provide a prisoner, thought Loring. This gift showed different paths through the vast Texas wilderness. It was invaluable, possibly a ticket home.

The map's topographical landmarks would be useful to find shelter, concealment, or the fastest route through the countryside. Loring paired this map with another of Louisiana.[1] The Louisiana map had been smuggled into camp by a Confederate German guard, and Loring had bartered with him for it. This contraband map provided the additional necessary information for a trek outside the gates of Camp Groce and ultimately to the safety of Union lines. The trick now would be to devise a strategy to escape from behind the walls of Camp Groce and to access an escape route quickly and quietly.

The escape needed to be carefully planned. Each night after dark, when the prisoners were confined to their meager quarters (no more than weather-worn sheds), Loring would stay up all night watching the sentries. He carefully observed the angles of possible approach to the prison walls—which provided the most cover and which could leave him exposed. He closely watched each guard to determine which were most vigilant and alert while on duty. During the day he noted which guards seemed to be amenable to bartering and trading with the prisoners, which he thought was an indication that they would be open to bribery. Loring watched for a fortnight through the cracks of the weather-beaten boards of the officers shed before he was satisfied he had gathered enough information to plan a run at the wall.

He knew that June 21, the darkest night of the month, would provide the best cover for an escape. To give this attempt the best possible chance at success, he began to experiment with rudimentary camouflage. Not one to trust anything to luck, he dressed one man in blue and another in gray and then instructed them to walk toward the sinks. Loring watched from his shed as the men walked away. The man wearing gray nearly melted into the night. Loring determined that "blue is decidedly distinct, grey is almost invisible."[2]

Subsequently Loring crafted a pair of crude pants from a gray blanket; while not the best sewn garment, it would suffice. With this portion of his escape wardrobe completed, the next challenge to consider was how to actually slip past the guards. The obvious solution was bribery. With most of their valuable possessions having been confiscated by the provost marshal for safekeeping, the prisoners had little to barter with. Not wanting to part with the few gold coins sewn into his trousers, Loring cut the buttons from one of his uniform coats that had been torn up from shot and shell during the battle of Calcasieu Pass. Selling these to several of the guards for $100 in Confederate currency, he would then use the money to bribe a guard to purchase a chance at freedom.[3]

By this point Loring had taken two kindred spirits into his confidence. Together they finalized their escape plans. Two nights before the escape a Union sailor from the *Wave* quietly crept to the proposed escape point at a corner of the stockade and dug around the base of a board, loosening it. The tall weeds inside the dead line hid the hole and the dirt piled nearby. The night of the escape Loring and his companions would pry the board loose, allowing them to crawl through and steal away.

On June 20 Loring approached a guard who he knew would be on sentry duty the night of the escape and bribed him with the Confederate money. The guard agreed to look the other way for a minute while in his guard box at the top of the stockade wall, which was one hundred feet from the point of escape. That would give Loring and the two other officers barely enough time to pry the loosened stockade board away and crawl through the wall. On June 21 at 11:15 p.m. the plan was put into action.[4]

Dressed in his gray camouflage trousers and dark jacket, Loring calmly crept from the officers' shed. Focusing on the space between it and the rear of the main shed, he crouched down. Staying low, he scrambled the forty yards from the officers' shed toward the edge of the enlisted men's shed. Reaching it, he slid to a stop. On hands and knees, with sweat beginning to drip from his forehead, he peered around the corner. What he saw was not part of his plan. Three men were attempting to scale a board that was propped up against the prison wall at a forty-five-degree angle.

The men were all trying to climb up the board and over the wall at the same time. The smooth, leather-soled brogans the men wore provided little traction. With so much weight on the board, it was beginning to bend under the strain and threatened to snap before any of the inmates could clear the top. The group was stymied, and in the open. Loring looked over his shoulder at the officers' shed and could see his two fellow escapees waiting for his signal to move.

The sentry at the top of the wall (the very same guard Loring had bribed) gesticulated and in forced whispers swore in Cajun French at the men below. The guard had been expecting Loring and two others to slip out. These unidentified Union prisoners now attempting to scale the stockade were mere feet away from the sentry, and even on this darkest of nights it was clearly evident that none of them was Loring. How would the escape of six men be explained in the morning? The Cajun guard waved his bayonet-tipped musket at the men, trying to deter them without drawing attention to his post.

With each passing moment the situation became more dangerous. The men were well within the ten foot dead line and at any time the guard could simply decide to end it all with a pull of the trigger. The deadly shot that would shatter the still night would alert the other sentries to fire in that direction, and all hell was sure to follow. Desperate to gain some traction on the board, the men adjusted the angle of it so it met the stockade wall four feet below the top. This decreased the angle, and the first man reached the top and was over. The second man waited until his comrade had cleared the top and then scrambled up and over. The third man glanced up at the guard and with a few quick movements made it to the top of the wall. With a flick of his foot he kicked the board away from the inner wall and was gone. All that could be heard was the blasphemous swearing from the guard. It was clear to Loring that this guard was in no mood for additional escape attempts that night.

Loring judged that it was better to wait for another opportunity to escape. On hands and knees he retreated to the corner of the officers' shed. It was not necessary to explain to his comrades what had happened, as they had witnessed the events as they unfolded. With nothing good to say about the situation, they would have to be patient and try again at a later date. The disappointment on each imprisoned sailor's face was evident as they parted ways. Loring wondered how much longer they could endure the deplorable conditions and when the next opportunity for escape would come.

Inside the officers' shed, Loring stripped off his homemade camouflage clothing and hid the garments under a floorboard. Lying down, he tried to sleep but kept wondering who the men were who had scaled the wall. As he drifted off to sleep he hoped they were well on their way to freedom, to once again report for duty.

With dawn and the inevitable roll call, it was soon discovered that three men were indeed missing. All three had managed to run off into the night. Freedom was theirs. It must have stung Loring to have come so close and not escaped. In the early morning light Loring looked around at his fellow officers. One was missing. It didn't take Loring long to realize who had escaped the previous night.

The news of the escape reached Colonel Gillespie. Furious, he enacted regulations to prevent any future escape attempts. He ordered that the guard be doubled, roll call would be taken a half hour after sunrise, and any man known to have aided an escape would be placed in irons. This was a punishment reserved for common criminals, not prisoners of war. Gillespie believed Loring knew about this escape attempt and had aided in its planning and execution. (If only he knew that Loring had meant to escape himself!) Intent on making life uncomfortable for Loring, Gillespie ordered Captain Odlum to report to him. Gillespie could barely contain his anger as he informed Odlum of his suspicions. In a fit of rage he told Odlum to make it hot for Loring.[5]

Several days later, with the beating of the drums, the men quickly assembled for roll call. With ranks formed and the men at attention, Captain Odlum, with an impressive number of guards accompanying him, made a grand entrance into the prison. Addressing the prisoners in his Irish brogue, Odlum made it very clear that should there be any further attempts to escape he had orders to clap Loring, the senior officer, in leg irons with ball and chain.

With the prisoners still in formation, the prison gates slowly swung open. Confederate guards with muskets leveled at the prisoners prodded three men in ragged, torn clothing through the opening. One day shy of a week since their escape, the worn-out escapees were returned to Camp Groce and put on display so all could see they had been recaptured.[6]

A sense of defeat washed over the men in the ranks as they watched their comrades enter the pen at bayonet point. Some wondered aloud if any of them would ever leave this place alive.

Loring saw the despair and hopelessness in the faces of his men. He grasped the opportunity to buoy their spirits and responded to Odlum, acknowledging that he was the senior officer in the prison and adding, "I accept the position and the entailing punishment. But, my men, it will give me immense satisfaction could every mother's son of you break away from these moorings. Go! And I will try to support the honor of the Union single-handed, and I shall also take pleasure in such a cause in wearing the glorious emblem of the Southern Confederacy; their disciplinary, civilizing ball and chain. Let no sentimental considerations for me stand between you and freedom. Remember this and God speed you on your way!"[7] He urged them to make their way to Union lines and report for duty. With a resounding "Huzzah for Lieutenant Loring," the men broke formation.

Loring recognized two of the recaptured men from the *Wave*, Ensign Howard and engineer Rogers. The third man was Lucius Harlowe, the assistant engineer from the *Granite City*. All three men were tired and scraped up but their spirits had not been broken. After being paraded about the prison they were incarcerated in the guardhouse, a form of solitary confinement.

Odlum's proclamation of punishment had the opposite effect from what he had hoped for. Frustrated, he muscled his way through the crowd toward the gates of the prison. Making his way out, Odlum spied a crude stool that Loring had cobbled together with nothing but a small ax loaned to him by a sentry. In a fit of anger Odlum called back to several of the guards, "Knock that damn bench to pieces!"[8]

The orders were promptly carried out.

10

Through the Wall

L oring longed for another opportunity to take a run at the wall. His two partners decided against risking their lives with another attempt. With the exception of the ill-fated escape of Howard, Rogers, and Harlowe, little of note had occurred since the night of June 21. And two months of confinement and boredom were beginning to take their toll.

Any personal items the prisoners had been allowed to keep had been traded to purchase food, medicine, or clothing to make life more bearable inside the prison camp. Anything of perceived value was used for trade and barter. Union uniform jacket buttons were as good as money and were sought after by the Confederate guards. Most of the guards were of German descent; they wore gray as victims of circumstances of geography rather than because they were Confederate sympathizers when the conflict began.[1] The prisoners carved small trinkets and figurines from beef bones, horns, or scraps of wood and traded them to the guards. Loring himself passed the time by crafting a powder horn from bone and some scrap metal. The prisoners' craft making became something of a cottage industry.

But it was the utter boredom of captivity that weighed most heavily on those confined. The daily grind of roll call and breakfast (what little there was of it) was followed by the mindless boredom of a long, hot day, then evening roll call, supper, and then, with sundown, renewed confinement in their sheds. With little outside stimulation, many of the men began to go stir crazy.

To keep his own mind sharp, Loring would play cribbage with fellow officers using a board and cards he had squirreled away in his sea chest. It was one of the few personal items that Loring had not traded away. There was also the daily discourse about the war's progress and whatever news might trickle in, as guards bragged about newspaper headlines in the *Galveston Daily News* proclaiming that the South was winning. Loring responded by simply stating that you couldn't trust the news from the *Galveston Daily Liar*.

During all of this Loring discreetly watched the guards and made mental notes. He shared his observations with his closest comrades as they planned an escape. Together they worked out the details and collected the materials they would need to survive on the outside. For two weeks, the men in Loring's mess contributed their ration of cornmeal to Loring. In the end he had enough to create two huge corn dodgers weighing nearly five pounds each.[2] These could be eaten on the run and would be the escape rations that sustained Loring and his comrades during their first four days on the outside.

But even as Loring made preparations, he was torn between his planned attempt at escape and his obligation to his men as senior officer in Camp Groce. He was devoted to his men, but if the opportunity arose for him to get out, he knew it was his duty to do so.

With conditions inside the pen declining daily, the prisoners and their clothing were now ragged and dirty. The stitching loosened on the men's trousers and belts needed to be tightened from lack of food. A few of the naval officers had been allowed to keep their sea chests in which they had an extra shirt or trousers. But by now, these articles of clothing and the trunks they were stored in had been traded for food for themselves and the enlisted men. This left most with only the clothing on their backs. This was stained, dirty, and threadbare from constant wear. Many clothes were more patches of material than the original garment. And even patching material had become so scarce that the men simply had no choice but to wear shirts with sleeves nearly torn off and trousers with huge holes in embarrassing places.

Since the first escape, the men were no longer allowed to travel outside the pen to bathe or wash their clothes in the stream. The only available water was from the single well inside the camp, which had been redug; this water was too precious to be wasted on washing. The stench emanated beyond the walls, so that a person could smell the human sewage from fifty feet outside the prison.

Holidays were eagerly anticipated as a break from the monotony of prison life. Plans to celebrate them were vigorously pursued as much as could be done behind prison walls. Even though there were no banquets or parades, the men came up with activities that might lift their spirits.

As June ended, the prisoners looked forward to celebrating the Fourth of July with speeches and patriotic songs. But soon enough, Colonel Gillespie caught wind of the prisoners' plans. On Independence Day he borrowed a regimental band to play the South's most patriotic melodies in order to spoil the day and antagonize the captives.[3]

After morning roll call on July 4, Loring and the several hundred men imprisoned in Camp Groce were treated to the rebel tunes floating across the top of the stockade walls. At first they ignored the offensive music and carried on with their speeches. But as the band's playing intensified they became more agitated. With their speeches entirely interrupted, the men began to compete with the band, breaking into song themselves.

As the band struck up "Dixie Land" and "The Bonnie Blue Flag" the Union men broke into "The Battle Hymn of the Republic." Several hundred Union voices together drowned out the five-piece rebel band and rallied the souls within the walls. As the song concluded, Loring led the men cheering in response to the offensive melodies with cries of "Here's to Lincoln! Three cheers for Grant! Hurrah for Farragut!"[4]

Throughout the day the band would try to play again, only to have their attempts drowned out by Loring's men. By midafternoon the band gave up and walked back to their camp. With Colonel Gillespie infuriated, Loring surmised he would crack down again.

Late that night, with the men inside their sheds, Loring and two others steeled their nerves as they readied for an escape. On the evening of July 3 the first part of the plan had been set in motion. In the early morning hours a naval quartermaster had quietly approached the prison wall where the escape attempt would be made. Hiding in the tall grass inside the dead line, he dug around the same board used during the previous escape. With the dirt loosened around the board, the escapees would only need to pry it from the wall to create an opening to squeeze through.

As dark descended upon Camp Groce, the celebrations of the Fourth concluded and the imprisoned men were once again confined to their sheds for the night. Loring and his escape partners rested and waited for the predetermined hour to make a run at the wall.

In preparation, Loring had assembled his escape kit. This included his hand-stitched gray camouflage pants, a red artillery cap, and a couple of regimental coat pins worn by Texas soldiers. Each of these items had been purchased with the Confederate money gained from the sale of his gold jacket buttons. He also had one of the huge corn dodgers. Not one to overlook any detail, Loring checked to make sure he had the most important item in his kit, which was carefully folded and tucked away in his spare trousers: a forged furlough pass.

This pass stated that Loring and his comrades were part of Gen. William Cook's artillery unit aboard the Confederate cotton-clad transport gunboat *J. F. Carr*, stationed at Matagorda, Texas.[5] The date on the forged pass was June 24, ten days overdue. This would help with the ruse that the men were Confederates who had not reported back promptly, a common case, as Confederates were often left to find their own way home to refit. While at home, Confederate soldiers would often work the fields and attempt to provide for their families, not knowing when they would be able to return again, if at all.

Since the previous escape Loring had several conversations with Harlowe and Rogers about their experience on the outside. These initial conversations had led to more intense and detailed discussions. Loring passed this hard-won information on to his escape partners.

But Loring's escape partners had grown weaker over the past month from lack of food and worsening conditions inside the prison. Just two days prior to the attempt, they told Loring they were too sick to make an escape. Rather than scrap the escape attempt, Loring approached Harlowe and Rogers themselves about coming with him. He knew that if these men were captured a second time, the consequences would be severe, perhaps even deadly. But Loring also knew his chances at a successful escape alone were very small. After a day of quiet but focused dialogue, the men agreed to break out in the early morning hours of July 5.

Studying the smuggled contraband maps of Texas and Louisiana, Loring had memorized a route that would lead to Matagorda Bay and freedom. After dark on the Fourth of July the plan moved forward.

Wearing his homemade Confederate uniform, Loring collected his kit. He carefully placed a rusty butter knife, a canteen, which unfortunately had a leak, and the five-pound corn dodger inside his uniform pants. He checked the pocket one more time for the forged pass and his trusty penknife, then rolled the pants up and tied them with a length of twine. He threw the kit over his shoulder onto his back and anxiously waited for the predetermined hour to rendezvous with Harlowe and Rogers.

At 11:20 p.m. Loring left the shed. Hunched over, he crept across the camp to the rendezvous point. He met Harlowe at the designated spot at the edge of the enlisted men's shed. Rogers was nowhere to be seen. After waiting what seemed an interminable time, they sent a message back to the officers' shed asking for Rogers. With no word of their comrade's whereabouts, Harlowe and Loring forged ahead.

Knowing they would be most vulnerable and visible while crossing the open ground toward the dead line, they crawled on hands and knees in the dirt and filth. They covered the 150 feet of open ground between the enlisted men's shed and the relative concealment of the tall grass inside the dead line near the prison wall. Harlowe's heavy breathing and less than stealthy scramble across the ground roused a sentry.

A young guard called out, "Who's there in the grass? Who's making that noise there? I'll shoot the top 'er your head off."[6] Keeping as still as possible, the two waited for a shot to ring out. The sentry, not sure if he actually had heard something, called out to his fellow guard one hundred feet away in the next guard box, "I heard a noise over there in the grass; didn't you?"[7]

His comrade, two hundred feet away from Loring and Harlowe, had not heard anything. The men waited for things to settle back down. With the sentry looking in the opposite direction, Loring again began to creep forward, motioning to Harlowe to do the same.

Crawling through the three-foot-high grass, they came to a point where the angle of approach required the utmost stealth because the sight lines of two guard boxes converged. They crawled next to the wall, where the grass was the tallest. Loring's hand-stitched gray trousers blended into the night.

Making it to the corner of the prison where the escape plank had been loosened, the men strained to listen. Both men grasped the board and gingerly pulled, testing to see how much force would be needed to further loosen it. The board wouldn't budge. The men tugged harder, trying to pry it away, but still it did not move.

Bracing themselves with their feet against the wall and hands on the board, they strained to pry the board loose. Suddenly there was a loud squeak as the square nails began to pull free from the horizontal boards holding it in place. The noise betrayed them and alerted the sentry. Peering into the night, the Confederate guard tried to see what had made the noise but could not see anything. With the board finally loosened, the time had come for Loring and Harlowe to squeeze through the wall.

Harlowe was the first to attempt to crawl through the narrow opening. Only it was too small. Loring tried to crawl through. Starved as he was from the meager prison diet of chicken feed and rancid bacon, he still could not squeeze his emaciated body through the wall. With a sweaty hand, Loring clawed at the rough bark, which made a rustling sound, further alerting the guard. "Hello, who's there? By hooky I'll shoot in that corner."[8]

The opening was just too small with the enormous five-pound corn dodgers on their backs. Taking their packs off, they tried to squeeze through the opening, but again to no avail. The situation was becoming more perilous as Loring and Harlowe continued to try and wedge themselves through the opening. The nearby sentry was becoming increasingly agitated, as he could hear something in the corner but could not see what was making the noise.

With the sentry's attention focused on their corner, Loring and Harlowe knew that further struggle would only provoke the guard to shoot in their direction. The two men took a moment to reconsider. After minutes of whispered discussion, they decided to wait for the changing of the guard. Then, instead of going through the wall, they would adjust the board to a forty-five-degree angle and shimmy up it, sliding over the wall—just as the sentry on duty climbed down from his guard box and the other sentry climbed up into the box. The timing had to be just right, but it seemed to be the only option left. The guard change occurred at midnight, leaving them a half hour to hug the corner and try to blend into the darkness.

Lying in the tall grass, Loring and Harlowe listened to the conversation between two of the guards. "Did you hear that? It sounds like there are cats running around in there."

"You must be hearing things."

"Come on, I know I heard something down there."

"Do you think any of those Yanks would try and escape? Colonel Gillespie would hang them if he caught them again. You don't think they are dumb enough to try that again, do you?"

"Well, better keep your eyes open. I'll put a neat hole through them if they try a run at the wall. Do you think it would take much lead to put one of them down?"[9]

The sentry suddenly stopped speaking and listened, cocking his head toward Loring and Harlowe's position. The two men held their breath. Not hearing anything, the sentry continued his banter. Loring and Harlowe slowly exhaled, their hearts beating so hard they thought their bodies would betray them. Harlowe was spooked, having lost half his hearing in both ears when a canon went off right next to him during the battle at Calcasieu Pass. He had tremendous difficulty discerning anything Loring was saying in hushed tones. Loring gave him a reassuring nod; all would be fine.

As the conversation between sentries continued, serendipity shone upon the two would-be escapees as one sentry called out to his comrade, "Do you remember the countersign, I forgot it. I think it was that Cavalry Colonel camped a few miles from here. What's his name?"

"It's 'Terry,' idiot, now shut up."

"Oh yeah, that's right."[10]

Now armed with the countersign should they need it, Loring and Harlowe waited for the changing of the guard and the moment when they could scramble up the loosened board and into the dark night. Their hearts pounded as they tried to control their breathing and calm down.

But Harlowe could take no more! Losing his nerve, he suddenly jerked up. Dropping his corn dodger, with a plaintive look at Loring, he ran back across the compound toward the officers' shed, covering the 150 feet in record time.

The sound of his running alerted the guard, who jerked his head in the direction of the sound. His musket came up and then he leveled it down into the camp, but he could not see anything.

"I heard something down in the pen and it is bigger than cats, I can tell you. I think it is one of them Yanks."

"I did not hear anything over here. Those Yanks aren't dumb enough to try and run at the wall again. It might be a hog got out."[11]

A minute later the call for the changing of the guard rang out. The sentry began to descend the steps of the wall. He commented to the man relieving him, "Thems some big goddamn rats running around in the pen. I bin hearing them all night. They bin causing some commotion down in there but I ain't bin able to see where they are."

Loring adjusted his pack, which now included both corn dodgers, and loosened the board again. Just as he was about to adjust it to a forty-five-degree angle, someone rushed up behind him on hands and knees! He instinctively grabbed the man and pulled him in close. Loring's eyes widened as he recognized Ensign Peter Howard. It was completely unexpected that some unknown person would come up behind him.

Very quietly, Howard explained that with word coming back to the officers' shed that Loring was looking for Rogers and with Harlowe's hasty reappearance at the enlisted men's shed, he knew something was afoot. It took Harlowe only a few words and gestures before Howard understood that Loring was making a run at the wall. With no forethought, no food, and not even a pair of shoes on his feet, Howard scrambled from the officers' shed and across the compound to find Loring in the corner of the wall. Howard was of French descent and had a decidedly French accent. Loring quipped to him that he was surprised at his appearance and called him a John Doe, or in his case Monsignor de Doe. The nickname stuck.

The opportunity to climb over the top of the wall at the changing of the guard was now lost. The newly posted sentry was in the guard box atop the wall just one hundred feet away. He would certainly see the board move away from the wall and would definitely see any man who might climb the board. The men would have to squeeze through after all.

With the board pulled away, de Doe went first. Young and lean, he squirmed, pushing his way through the gap, scraping his chest and back. Loring passed the two corn dodgers and his kit out to him. Now it was his turn.

Lying on his side, his arms outstretched above him, Loring first squeezed his head through. On the other side, de Doe grabbed Loring's arms, and with bare feet braced against the outside of the wall, he pulled. Loring kicked and struggled. His chest and ribs scraped on the rough-hewn sides of the adjacent boards as he snaked through the wall. Loring was bruised and cut, but he was out! Reaching back through the wall, Loring pulled the board back into its proper position. On the outside, the damp grass and cool night air greeted them. With no one in sight and the nearest sentry's attention focused inside the pen, they stole into the fresh and freeing darkness.[12] As Loring took his first few steps toward freedom in more than two months, he thought of his family. But to be reunited with them once again would require his iron resolve to make it back to Union lines and report for duty.

11

On the Outside

After gathering themselves next to the wall, Loring and de Doe sprinted to a small brook nearby. They stopped for only a minute to clean some of the larger abrasions on their arms and chests and to wash away the rank stench of the prison, with the idea that if the dogs were set upon them, it would make the task of tracking them more challenging.[1] The cool water offered a welcome respite, but there was no time to enjoy it.

Loring surveyed the clear night sky. He calculated the direction based on the visible stars, setting a course for the Brazos River. A ship's captain, Loring had navigated by the stars across the vast oceans, so finding their way across land would not be a problem. De Doe, less adept at astronomical navigation, followed wordlessly, thankful for Loring's company on such a deadly adventure.

After just ninety minutes of walking and still within five miles of the prison walls, de Doe's lack of footwear put the entire escape in jeopardy. His bare feet were scraped and bruised, and trickles of blood smeared his soles. Stumbling in the dark, he had stubbed his toes several times on rocks and small stumps. He needed to stop and improvise some kind of a covering for his feet or he would not be able to walk much farther. Loring wanted to put as much distance between themselves and the prison as possible before sunrise but realized that neither man would get much farther if they did not attend to de Doe's vulnerable feet.

Stopping to rest, Loring removed his gray camouflage trousers. He unrolled his regular uniform pants (which he had used to carry the escape kit and corn dodgers) and put them on. Pulling out his small bone-handled penknife, he cut the handmade trousers into long sections. He wrapped these around de Doe's feet, swaddling them like a newborn baby. This would provide some protection and allow the men to increase their pace.

Soon they were back on the trail. Twenty minutes later, de Doe was bent over, adjusting the wrappings, when Loring noticed that something was amiss. De Doe seemed as if he had shrunk. "De Doe, what happened to your corn dodger?" "By the great Napoleon! I forgot it where we last stopped to fix my feet."[2]

Loring was not a man to let such incompetence go unnoticed or unaddressed, but in this circumstance, a scowl was all that was needed to convey his extreme disappointment. De Doe understood that such gross negligence would not be tolerated. Half of their precious provisions were lost and they were not yet ten miles from the prison camp; such sloppiness could not continue if they were to be successful. The remaining corn dodger would now have to sustain them both in the coming days.

Loring had studied the maps of Texas and Louisiana in the days prior to the escape. He had memorized a route that used the rivers and forests to their advantage during their trek to freedom. His planned route provided for swift and easy travel on the rivers, and when necessary it would keep them tucked inside the forests to avoid encounters with the local citizenry, who could betray them.

But to reach the rivers in the Texas low country they would first have to traverse swamps and bayous. These swampy lowlands provided the cover they sought but impeded any type of fast travel cross-country. Slogging through the swamps, the men waded through water that varied in depth from ankle to waist deep. With each step the Texas mud sucked at their legs, draining their energy.

As the sun slowly broke through dense clouds on the first day of the escape, the men found themselves on the edge of a wide plantation field. Taking a moment to survey their surroundings, Loring scanned the distance while de Doe adjusted his foot wraps. The distinctive high-pitched sounds of a slave calling his hogs could be heard nearby. Loring noted the general direction of the voice and began to pick his way through the thick underbrush on the edge of the field for a better view.

From a well-concealed position, Loring and de Doe scanned the immediate area. Two hundred yards away a Negro was walking parallel to their location. They waited to make sure that he was alone and then stepped out into the field and carefully approached. The slave was startled to see Loring and de Doe suddenly appear from the brush but waited for them to come close. Through some guarded questions and answers by both parties, Loring determined that the Brazos River was just a few miles away. Further questioning led to specific directions: "You can get there quickest by following that fence."[3] Loring smiled. The fact that navigable water was close by lifted the Union sailors' spirits, and they pressed on.

During the past several weeks, torrential rains had beset the area; subsequently, the Brazos River had overflowed its banks and flooded the low-lying areas of the upper Gulf Coast of Texas. The men followed a fence toward the river, walking in chest-deep water. In an attempt to stay dry, they straddled the top fence rail and tried to push themselves along it to stay out of the deepest water. The rough split-rail fence cut into their backsides, and this method of travel helped little and slowed their progress dramatically. The pair decided that rapid travel was preferable to staying dry, so they simply slogged on through the water. There was nothing they could do to avoid the muddy floodwaters of the Brazos.

The river itself was still an hour away, but the land was so low and flat that river waters had no obstacles, spreading out to the horizon. By the time Loring and de Doe reached the river itself they were tired, cold, and soaked through. They stood knee deep in water on the flooded banks of the actual river. Staring out across the swift-moving, muddy waters, they were dismayed to discover that the road they needed to follow continued on the opposite side.

Like a caged animal, de Doe paced back and forth along the riverbank, staring at the other side. Loring watched as de Doe took a few hesitant steps toward the drop-off into the river, then backed away, walking up a few yards to try another spot and backing off again. Walking back over to Loring, de Doe stopped. He looked Loring squarely in the eye and confessed that he could not swim but said he would learn right then and there in order to win his freedom.

Loring was a strong swimmer, having spent many childhood days in Duxbury, Massachusetts, enjoying the local swimming hole. He also knew that trying to swim across a flooded river with unpredictable currents was not the best way for his partner to learn how to swim. He complimented de Doe on his resolve but dissuaded him from any attempt.

Loring was sure they could cross the river without getting wet. They would just need to locate a boat and borrow it. Loring headed upriver and de Doe went downriver, searching for a boat. They searched the riverbank for half a mile each way with no luck. With the day's light dimming under dense clouds, the men had walked, waded, and skulked through flooded forests and muddy swamps. They had skirted around several small cabins, family farms, and wealthy plantations and were dog tired. They would have to continue the search for a boat the following day.

The two settled on a soggy hummock barely eight feet square and less than six inches above the floodwaters and made camp for the night. Loring unwrapped the remaining corn dodger and broke off a couple of ounces, passing them to de Doe. Cold and wet, the men huddled together and ate their small ration like half-drowned mice nibbling on a crust of bread. With the darkness of night upon them, a buzzing sound began to grow as the blood-sucking denizens of the swamp emerged.

The swarms of mosquitos were as thick as smoke. Loring and de Doe cut swaths through the hordes of tiny insects as they waved their arms to keep them at bay. The mosquito's villainous partner in torture, a sort of chigger, emerged as well. These tiny bugs crawled up the pant legs and onto the backs of both men, biting them and causing a terrible itching sensation; scratching them left small bleeding pockmarks on their skin.

Loring swung his arms about him in an attempt to ward off the mosquitos and swatted at his pants to keep the invading chiggers from biting his hide. But de Doe was just too exhausted to fight them—seemingly impervious to the insects, he had curled up and was fast asleep. In an attempt to keep from being sucked dry, Loring swatted at the bugs throughout the night.

The following morning the sun's heavily filtered beams shone through the clouds. Loring roused de Doe and they continued their search for a boat. Together the men walked a mile downriver in waist-deep water along the river's flooded, brushy edge. They came upon the remains of an old cabin that appeared to have been a ferry crossing. As they poked around the remnants of the building, they heard the sounds of early morning drift toward them. At first it was just birds, then a few dogs barking in the distance, and then the voices of the local plantation inhabitants, as the men and women bound to these huge farms began to rise and start their day. The proximity of the plantation added to the threat that some poor soul might happen along and spot the fleeing Union sailors. Loring wanted to give these domiciles a wide berth, but doing so meant that they would need to push deep into the thick cane fields that surrounded the Texas plantations.

To avoid the possibility of being discovered by the local inhabitants Loring led the way into the head-tall cane. The sugar cane provided the concealment they sought, but it was difficult to get through. They could not see more than a few feet ahead, and travel in a straight line was nearly impossible. After an hour of trying to push their way through the jungle of sugarcane, they backtracked to the forest.

As they rested, de Doe readjusted his foot wrappings and Loring considered their next move. Loring looked to the sky, but the steel-gray clouds hid the sun. Without a compass and with no visible sun, Loring could not determine with any certainty what direction they were headed in. Having braved many stormy seas and battles in the past, he was not deterred by this challenge and decided that the best course of action was to let the currents of the river guide them to their destination.

The forest provided all the materials they would need to construct a raft. The two men pulled together several small logs for the base of the hull and used grapevines to tie these together. With no tools with which to actually cut or shape the logs, it took most of the day to build. After much effort and expenditure of energy the small raft was completed.[4] As another day drew to an end they launched the raft into the muddy waters of the Brazos River.

The raft itself resembled a floating pile of debris that had collected against the piling of a bridge. When the men pushed the raft into the water and attempted to climb aboard their weight caused the whole mess to sink several inches below the surface. The buoyancy of the raft was not enough to support them out of the water. With most of their belongings on board, Loring and de Doe would hang onto opposite sides, and with both men kicking they would propel the crude raft across the river.

The last item left to take was the one remaining corn dodger. Loring and de Doe stared at the five-pound dodger, contemplating how to keep it dry during the river crossing. The only thing that might be out of the water during the entire crossing was Loring's head.[5] So Loring took the dodger and placed it right there. The men pushed the raft into the current and began to swim.

Loring deftly balanced the precious corn dodger on his head. After a half hour of paddling, floating, and maneuvering they struck shallow water on the opposite side of the Brazos near another cane field. Loring carefully removed the corndodger from his head. The men gathered their belongings and melted into the thick, ten-foot-tall jungle of sugarcane.

Pushing through the cane field and some shallow sloughs, they found an abandoned road leading them through a low-lying, forested swamp to a small stream. Once again the Brazos River had wound back on itself. Taking a moment to rest and consider their options, Loring looked about for materials to build another raft. Though tired and anxious to keep moving, de Doe refused to build another raft. Adjusting his foot wraps, he told Loring that he would "swim or drown in the attempt."[6]

With the decision made to swim across the river, Loring stripped off his clothes and laid them on the shore. On the first trip across he would take the escape kit and the corndodger. He would come back for his clothing and would help de Doe across on the second trip. Again he pressed the corn dodger onto his head. With his escape kit tied up and slung over his back, he waded into the cold waters of the Brazos.

Mid-river, Loring began to struggle to keep his head above water. Five pounds of corn dodger felt like fifty. Swimming another seventy-five yards, he could barely keep his nose above the water. The weight of the dodger on his head and the drag of the escape kit on his back became too much to manage, and he went under. With a surge of adrenaline and a couple of powerful strokes, Loring managed to break the surface and gasped for air. The corn dodger increased in weight as it acted like a sponge, soaking up water.

Loring went under again as the weight of the dodger bore down on him. Barely able to make it back to the surface a second time, he had to make a decision—toss a soggy corn dodger or drown. With the flick of his head, the corn dodger was thrown aside. Treading water, Loring saw that he had underestimated the width of the river. He turned around and swam back. Reaching shore, Loring dragged his shivering body from the river and dressed in his ragged Confederate clothing. They would have to find an alternative to swimming across this wide section of the Brazos.

Both men sat on the riverbank's only dry spot. Hungry and tired, Loring could only think of the corn dodger floating downriver. Standing up, he undressed one more time and waded into the water to locate and retrieve it. Swimming nearly 250 yards, he found the corn dodger, floating like an iceberg. Grabbing it, he pushed it out ahead of himself as he swam back to shore. Reaching the shore, he rolled the waterlogged lump of corn mush onto the bank. Realizing that it was no longer edible, he looked at de Doe and disgustedly threw it back into the river.

As Loring dried off and dressed, de Doe scanned their surroundings and mentioned to Loring that there was something familiar about them. Loring looked about and noticed the remains of an old cabin that resembled a ferry crossing.[7] He too thought it seemed familiar. At the same moment both men realized that they had returned to the same place they had been the previous day! Somehow they had become turned around, recrossed a shallow section of the river without realizing it, and ended up where they began. Loring was perturbed and disappointed with himself. Navigating at night under cloudy skies with no visible stars or compass to guide them, they had moved in a circle. They would have to backtrack four miles to reach the road and begin again. Loring was furious with himself for making such a mistake.

The four-mile walk back through waist-deep water and the jungles of cane fields took two hours as the sun was dimming on the cloudy second day of the escape. Hungry and weary, the men hid in the brush. As night fell, the bloodthirsty mosquitos once again emerged. Seeking some kind of relief from the bugs, Loring recalled including a small tin of tallow in his kit. He smeared this on his body with the hope that it might prove impervious to the mosquitos or at least relieve the itching of the chiggers. The tallow did provide a little protection from the mosquitos, and it caused the chiggers to loosen their grip. With his penknife, Loring scraped his legs and arms, which seemed to provide some relief.[8]

Loring's suffering did not end with the bugs and chiggers, though. His feet were severely blistered. Slogging through the water for the past couple of days, his rough leather shoes had caused his socks to bunch up, allowing the leather to rub against his skin. Loring limped the last two miles and after inspecting his feet discovered that the blisters were so severe that two of his toenails were now loose and threatening to fall off.[9] He turned to ask de Doe how his foot wraps were holding up, but de Doe was already asleep.

In the brush alongside the road, Loring was unable to sleep, so he watched for a suitable passerby to approach for directions. Hearing the clomping of a team of oxen, Loring peered through the brush. Just before the teamster came around the bend, he jumped up on the road. To pull off the ruse of being a Confederate soldier headed home on furlough, he twirled his canteen and softly whistled "Way Down South in Dixie." He called out to the teamster as he pulled alongside, walking and talking with the man as he asked for directions. After a few carefully phrased questions he discovered that a small town, Bellville, was about nine miles away. Loring pressed for further information without trying to rouse any suspicion. The teamster, clearly done answering questions from this stranger, adjusted his broad-brimmed hat and increased the pace of his mules, pulling ahead and out of sight. Loring jumped back into the brush. He was now sure they were on the correct road and headed in the right direction.

At dawn Loring woke de Doe and the two men gathered their belongings. Staying inside a cornfield to avoid detection, they moved parallel to the road. Despite de Doe's constant need to adjust his foot wraps and Loring's blistered feet, they were able to make good time.

The heat was oppressive, even with the skies overcast. They needed to find some water to quench what had become a tremendous thirst. Coming upon a small house along the road, the two sailors stopped to drink and fill their canteen. The cool well water had a musty smell but easily slid down their throats. They again began to move through the countryside, until the heat of the day forced them to find more water. Locating none along the road, they decided to head to the river to slake their thirst.

As they moved through the bottomlands they became infested with beggar-lice, small hook-like seeds from a local plant. When an animal or person rubs up against the seed, its little hook latches onto the passerby and it is thereby transported until it falls off and the plant germinates from the seed. A rather ingenious design on nature's part. Walking through a field of these plants it is easy to become covered in the seeds, with the little hooks grabbing clothing and bare skin. They seemed to find their way into the cracks and crevices of the human body, where they became particularly irritating.

The men reached the banks of the river and drank their fill from the torpid waters. De Doe adjusted his foot wraps. Loring untied his boots and loosened the laces. He winced as he gingerly took off his boots and socks to reveal his wet, withered feet, raw with blisters.

Sitting on a log to rest, Loring reached into his pocket and pulled out his small penknife. It was just three inches in length with the blade closed but had proved itself useful many times over. He opened the blade and recalled the day his sister Lillie put it in his hand as he was preparing to leave and report for duty at the Washington Navy Yards. That small bone-handled knife had been his constant companion ever since. He pulled his trousers taut and used the flat of the blade to scrape the beggar lice from each pant leg and then his jacket.

He was a sight to see, and not a fair one. He had not slept in three nights and was hungry as a bear and covered in beggar lice, with mosquito bites and scratches all over him from which oozed little streamlets of blood. He was covered with the grease of the tallow and his severely blistered feet were now missing two toenails. His clothing was in tatters and hanging from his feverish skeleton underneath. His physical condition was quickly deteriorating, and there were many miles yet to travel before he could report for duty. They had already endured so much. Both men slumped on the ground and quietly wondered how much more suffering lay ahead.

On the Outside

Plantations

Having had nothing to eat in thirty-six hours, Loring's strength was sapped and it took a herculean effort just to stand up. With some words of encouragement, he prodded de Doe to do the same. Loring was committed to report for duty and reminded de Doe that they must press on. Drawn and gaunt, the two men began walking. Throughout the day their pace became slower and slower as they became drained of energy. As evening approached the pair followed a fence row that led to an enormous plantation. Loring knocked on the door of the house. A stout black woman answered and actually gasped at the sight of the two ragged men. A white woman followed, looked at Loring, and matter-of-factly asked, "What do you want?"[1] Loring, in something of a Southern accent, asked if they could please spare some food for two poor soldiers. The reply was a curt "No!" Loring turned and shuffled down the stairs. As he reached de Doe at the bottom a slave hissed at them from around the corner of the house and motioned for them. He handed a small, dirty cloth to Loring. Having overheard his mistress's response, this kind soul gave what little he had to share, a small portion of cornbread and an even smaller piece of bacon. Considering that Loring was dressed as a Confederate soldier, this was no small act of charity. The small ration did little to satisfy the men's hunger but lifted their spirits. Loring and de Doe gobbled up the food where they stood and inquired about where they might stop for a proper meal. Hesitant, the black man said that they could cross the large field, continue straight, and that would lead them to a local judge. He would be sure to provide them with some food. Loring and de Doe thanked this kind soul and struck out for the judge's home.

It was a difficult decision. As the men drank from the judge's well and topped off their canteen they stared down the long lane leading to the judge's plantation. They weighed the risk of whether to stop and ask for some food and run the chance of being discovered as escaped Union prisoners. Their stomachs certainly wanted to take the risk, but not wanting to press their luck with an encounter with the judge, they moved on.

By midnight they stumbled upon a stream that at first they thought was the Brazos River again. As they struggled and pushed along through the brush-choked waterway the ever-present swarms of mosquitos added to their misery. Breaking off a few leafy branches, they flailed at the hordes of mosquitos, trying to fend them off. Throughout the night the men followed the meandering water, forcing their way forward. The tangle of undergrowth, scrub brush, and briers tore their clothing and scratched at their skin. Hour after hour they pressed on through the jungle. As a new day dawned they stumbled upon a ford in the stream. The welcome break in the brush presented them with an opportunity to cross. The respite was short-lived. Reaching the opposite side, a vast sunbaked prairie spread out before them as far as they could see.

The sun rose above the horizon in a cloudless sky for the first time in three days. Loring shaded his eyes with his hand as he looked up and noted the position of the sun. Turning to de Doe, he confidently stated, "This way" and led a southwesterly course toward the San Bernard River.[2]

The open prairie was a relief from the swamp; it provided a long, clear field of view. But there was no cover to avoid encounters with the locals. With little to impede their progress other than their own failing bodies, they took advantage of the flat terrain and pressed on. The opportunity to move quickly was short-lived, as Loring's hip began to bother him. The severe blistering of his feet had caused him to walk awkwardly for the past day. This had a cumulative effect. Over the course of many miles it had caused Loring's body to put undue pressure on his hip joints. Limping along, his leg would at times give out altogether, causing him to fall. De Doe was in a similar condition. Every half mile the men would briefly stop and de Doe would adjust his foot wrappings.

As the two men staggered across the prairie, they found themselves in the midst of hundreds of wild cattle scattered across the range. As the men moved through the herd several of the bulls became agitated. The huge beasts would paw at the dirt and then move in close, swinging their massive horned heads in warning. The men shuffled along as quickly as their blistered feet could carry them, looking back over their shoulders every few steps.

Loring commented to de Doe that Texas seemed to be a land of extremes. First too much water, now there was none. In this parched land, potable water was not readily found, and the leaky canteen needed constant refilling. Thirst became an issue as the sunbaked prairie began to take its toll. The desolate landscape was dotted with small depressions where the cattle had wallowed. The putrid pits collected stagnant water and most certainly contained a brew of microscopic tormentors. But in desperate need of water, they sank to their knees and with cupped hands scooped up the scum-covered soup and drank.[3]

By midafternoon the heat became nearly unbearable and the men struggled to stay upright. The midday mirage on the horizon played tricks on the men's eyes. Seemingly vast lakes of water appeared before them only to evaporate as quickly as they appeared. Loring strained, looking to the horizon for any sign of water or relief from the sun. He saw what first appeared as tiny dots, but as they moved closer the dots turned into shimmering brown shapes. Loring was unsure what these were and expected that they would disappear just like all the other mirages that had danced before them. But as the men came within a couple hundred yards it was clear that this was a copse of trees. Loring rubbed his eyes. Yes, trees! A tiny oasis that might hold some water or at the very least provide some relief from the solar devil.

Reaching the shade, there was immediate relief from the heat. Desperately they searched for any puddle or rivulet of water but found none. Loring kicked at the dry, sandy soil. A darker layer of soil was revealed. He kicked again. The soil was darker still. His throat too dry to speak, he pointed. De Doe fell to his knees and began to scrape at the dirt with his hands. Loring knelt down and grabbed a small stick and stabbed at the dirt. Inch by inch the dirt became darker and then cooler. The deeper they dug the darker it became. Rubbing their fingers raw, they continued to excavate. At a depth of eight inches the sides of the little hole began to show a few drops of water. At a depth of ten inches the slightest trickle of water began to fill the bottom of the hole. For the next two hours the men laid next to the life-saving hole and took turns lapping up the earthy tasting water and thanking god they had found it.

With the worst of their thirst relieved, Loring and de Doe had a renewed sense of energy. They each scampered up the trunk of a nearby tree, and from this perch they scanned the flat, open horizon. Barely visible, several miles away, they could see the outline of a house. In dire need of a meal and more water, they set a course toward it. Arriving at dusk, the men walked up to the gate, calling out a friendly hello to make their presence known. Mr. Johnson, a cattleman of Mexican descent, looked up from his work in the yard at the approach of unfamiliar voices.

Smiling, Loring launched into a tale of two Confederate artillerymen on furlough heading home to refit. Johnson eyed the men suspiciously, but Loring did not miss a beat. Finally convinced that they were indeed Confederates on furlough, Johnson invited them to supper.[4] Between bites of beef and large amounts of fresh cornbread, Loring kept up a jaunty conversation. De Doe just smiled between mouthfuls. Once the dinner plates were emptied of their contents, Johnson invited the men to stay for the evening. With full stomachs, both men stretched out on the floor in front of the fireplace. Sleep came quickly.

The next morning, Loring and de Doe awoke to the sounds of the ranchers starting their day. They took advantage of their host's hospitality and enjoyed a hearty breakfast. While watching the vaqueros go about their work on the ranch, Loring noticed various discarded scraps of hides lying about the yard. As de Doe wrapped his feet in preparation to begin the day's walk, Loring had an idea. It occurred to him that he might fashion some footwear for de Doe from these scraps. Gathering several larger pieces of hide, Loring cobbled together a pair of moccasins for de Doe using what was left of the trouser wraps to tie the hides around his feet. De Doe could not have been more pleased if these had been brand-new calfskin boots. With the moccasins completed, they thanked Johnson for his hospitality and resumed their trek toward the San Bernard River.

Plantations

Loring's sore hip continued to cause him difficulty, and it became worse as the day wore on. After several hours of limping along, the outline of distant trees marked a river channel. Reaching the riverbank, the thirsty men were dismayed to find a dry basin where the San Bernard River should have been. They were forced to move on. A mile farther on they located a house. The owner, a rebel soldier of German heritage, graciously filled their canteen as they swapped information. Loring was polite but cautious and shared little.

With the approach of evening, the men came to Alleyton.[5] They had traveled over fifty miles south of Camp Groce and were now seventy miles due west of Houston. Having fooled Johnson into believing that they were Confederate soldiers on furlough, they were quite confident in their ability to blend in. Loring quipped to de Doe that his own mother would not recognize him. Rather than skirt the town, they would walk right down the main street with the local inhabitants. They passed shops and locals with no one suspecting that the two ragged soldiers were escaped Yankee prisoners on a freedom march. No one even glanced at them sideways.

At the opposite end of town, Loring stopped a slave and ascertained that the Columbus Ferry was nearby. He also learned that there was at least one sentry posted on the near side of the Colorado River and that a signed pass was required for passage across. This information was important. Further discussion led to an alarming discovery. Encamped on the opposite side of the river was an entire division of three thousand Confederate troops ready to handle any situation that might come up.

Loring and de Doe wasted no time leaving the town. Carefully, they made their way toward the river. They stuffed themselves into the thickest brush they could find on the riverbank. Listening, they could hear the voices of the troops drifting across the water. As the moon rose the outline of the ferry, secure in its moorings, was silhouetted. Without a signed pass there was no hope of crossing. They moved downriver in search of a shallow ford where they could cross. De Doe spotted a section where the inner river had slowed, depositing mud and sand to create a bar that extended out into the river. Keeping low, they moved out onto the spit of sand to make for the other side below the rebel encampment.

De Doe wasted no time, stripping off his clothing and moving toward the water. Loring heard a rush of rapids. Realizing what waited for them around the bend, he tried to dissuade de Doe from trying to swim across. De Doe would hear nothing of it. "By the great Napoleon! I will swim or drown!"[6] Venturing into the cool, swift waters, de Doe struggled. Loring followed. Once de Doe was chest deep in the water he suddenly disappeared in the current. Losing sight of de Doe in the dark, Loring stopped, waist deep, and strained to listen for his compatriot above the rush of the water. Making it to the opposite side of the river, Loring stood, looking up at the twelve-foot-high banks. There was no way he could climb up and out of the river. Pausing, he again listened, hoping to hear any sound that meant that de Doe was still alive.

Loring's head snapped around as the sound of a splash downriver caught his attention. In a loud whisper he called out to de Doe. "Goddamnit" was the response. This reply was not to Loring's liking. De Doe cursed again and called back to Loring. He had made it across but was stuck in chest-deep water. De Doe stood on several large pieces of clay that had fallen from the bank above. Trying to find a way up the steep bank, he slipped off the clay chunks and was swept farther downriver. Flailing about, trying to keep his head above water, he finally found a foothold and dragged himself up the nearly seven-foot vertical bank. Safe on the riverbank, he shouted to Loring that he had found a way up and was now on dry land. Loring surfed the current downstream, found the clay chunks, and clawed his way up the bank.

Dressed in their ragged clothing again, de Doe discovered that in his haste he had left his moccasins on the other side, upriver.[7] Loring stared at de Doe in utter disbelief. De Doe could not possibly continue on without the moccasins, nor could he swim back to retrieve them. Without a word, Loring undressed. He slid back into the river and disappeared. All de Doe could do was sit and wait. Fifteen minutes became thirty. Thirty minutes dragged by to forty-five. De Doe paced the edge of the riverbank, straining to catch any sound of Loring swimming back. Loring had been gone nearly an hour. De Doe was sure that his comrade had slipped beneath the Colorado River and had been washed away. How could he have been so careless as to forget the moccasins?

A splash fifty feet downriver caught de Doe's attention. There were some rustling sounds in the brushy grass. De Doe crouched down. Whatever it was, was slowly making its way toward him. Just twenty feet away the outline of something crawling appeared. It was Loring! Covered in mud from crawling up the bank and with the moccasins secured around his waist, Loring collapsed in the grass. He was completely spent. His hip was so sore and lame that he could no longer lift his leg; he could barely drag it behind him. De Doe helped Loring get dressed and thanked him over and over for retrieving the moccasins. Loring admonished his partner and made him swear to never again forget them.

Giving the division of three thousand Confederates encamped along the Colorado River a wide berth, the bedraggled pair moved on. Exhausted, they camped for the night out of earshot of the Confederate force.

13

Dog Ranch

A bugle burst the serenity of the early morning of July 10 as the first rays of dawn broke over the horizon. De Doe leapt up so suddenly it appeared he had never slept at all. The sound of the bugle faded as the sounds of three thousand Confederates beginning their day wafted toward the startled men. "Rise and shine, here! Sorry to disturb your nap, but life is short, liberty sweet, and there's a hornet's nest close aboard," Loring quipped.[1] The men rolled up their few possessions in their blankets and quickly moved. They had completely misjudged their proximity to the rebel camp on the outskirts of Columbus, Texas, the previous night.

The bugle blast cast no doubt as to just how close they had unknowingly come to walking into the middle of this rebel encampment. Loring and de Doe quickly hobbled off, putting some distance between themselves and the Southern soldiers on the sixth day of their escape.

After a two-mile march, they found a house, inquired within for some breakfast, and after some very hard negotiating were allowed a meager ration. While downing some cornbread, Loring looked up and saw a young man no more than sixteen years of age standing in the doorway glaring at de Doe. Eating quickly, they asked a few vague questions regarding the Petersburg road and moved on, not wanting any trouble. Discerning the direction of travel, Loring led the way. They would head toward the Navidad River and a small town called Boxville.[2]

With the heat of the day quickly becoming oppressive, Loring and de Doe pressed on. The men needed to locate water every five to seven miles, so they moved from well to well throughout the day. As evening descended, the men found a house near the road and asked for some cornbread. They enjoyed the fresh bread and rested as the sun set. Just a half mile farther down the road in the open prairie, the men encountered clouds of gallinippers. Half an inch in length and with serrated jaws, these vicious insects descended on the men with a vengeance. The insects stabbed through their tattered clothing, inflicting extraordinarily painful bites.

Nearly defenseless against the hordes of insects, they waved their caps in the air and cut a swath through the clouds of the biting beasts. They battled their way across the prairie for four hours. As they reached the edge of some woods the onslaught subsided.

Just inside the woods was another dry Texas riverbed. As they searched for water, a nearby dog heard the noise and investigated. Moving closer, the dog smelled the men and its hackles stood up on its back. Baring its teeth, it growled at Loring and began to bark. The dog was joined and echoed by another and then still another until a full pack of dogs descended upon Loring and de Doe.[3] As the pack of dogs grew larger they became more brazen. Growling with teeth bared, they circled, lunging and barking. Loring and de Doe tried to move away as quickly as possible but Loring's bad leg prevented him from running. Trying to defend himself from the pack of frenzied animals, Loring reached into his pocket and pulled out his small penknife. Hardly the weapon of choice, it was his only defense. De Doe grabbed a large stick and swung it about him as a chase ensued. Trying to keep a tree between themselves and the pack, they scrambled to try and keep from being overrun and bitten.

The dogs rushed in, jumping at the men trying to knock them down. De Doe struggled to stay on his feet as he tried to draw the animals away from Loring, who limped from tree to tree. In the distance, the dim flicker of a candle could be seen in a house window. They headed toward this possible safe haven.

Limping and stumbling along, the men kept moving toward the safety of the house. The encounter with the pack of dogs had turned into a running battle. De Doe battered one dog but another swung around behind him and narrowly missed sinking its teeth into his backside. He swung the thick branch around again and caught another dog across its snout. It yelped as blood flowed from its nose. With the scent of blood in the air the pack was further enraged. Loring sliced at the dogs with his little penknife, keeping the trunk of the nearest tree between himself and the closest dogs. They reached the ramshackle house with the blood-thirsty dogs at their heels. Loring yelled out, "Let us in!" A raspy, unfriendly response came back with, "Who the hell is out there?" With the dogs still barking, growling, and lunging, Loring yelled out again, "Let us in!" Loring swung his good leg and the toe of his boot caught one of the dogs in the ribs. It yelped as it rolled off the porch of the shack.

A few footsteps could be heard inside the small house and the door opened just a crack. The owner of the home wanted to know who they were, what in god's name they wanted, and why they had stirred up the local dogs in the middle of the night.

Loring pleaded with the man to call off the pack of dogs. The old man let loose with a torrent. "You goddamn, flea-bitten sons o' bitches, shut up! Shut up! Bastards." The dogs stopped barking, tucked their tails between their legs, and skulked away.

With the dogs now quiet, the old man demanded to know who Loring and de Doe were and why they were raising hell in the middle of the night. Loring, in his now-practiced tone, explained that they were Confederate soldiers on furlough and were in need of some water. The man did not let it go and asked again, "What are you doing here causing such a commotion?" Loring did his best to explain that they were soldiers on furlough and were heading back home by way of Boxville.

The old man folded his arms. He was sure they were Confederate deserters. Loring retorted that if they were deserters, why would they be causing such a ruckus and stopping to ask for water. Not entirely convinced, the old man brought them a pitcher of water. Quickly drinking the entire pitcher, Loring asked for some more. The old man filled their canteen. Loring and de Doe made a speedy exit with the old man still muttering to himself.

Just as Loring and de Doe reached the edge of the forest a deep voice yelled out, "Stop right there! Get back here and let's see those passes."[4] They were only a few feet from the safety of the forest. De Doe didn't have the strength to run and Loring was barely able to walk. Turning around, they hobbled back to the house. A young man in his twenties stood in the doorway and demanded, "Let's see those passes."

Opening a small leather pouch, Loring reached in and pulled out an oiled cloth. Inside the cloth, neatly folded, was the forged pass. Loring stepped closer to the young man. As he held out the precious piece of paper he saw the gaping muzzle of a revolver pointed at his chest. Grabbing the pass from Loring, the man looked it over, pointing to various parts of the document with the muzzle of the gun. Several other men were now standing in the doorway. One man in particular towered above all the others. Holding a candle to shed some light on the passes, he peered at the documents over the shoulders of the men in front of him. After what seemed an eternity came the verdict. The man with the gun declared to the others that the papers were good. Loring calmly responded, "Yes they are. Why would we have them if they weren't any good?" De Doe stood with his mouth agape and stared.

The examining party mentioned that if they were forgeries they were quite well done. The old man, still suspicious, asked, "Who are you going to see at Boxville?" Loring deadpanned, "Harry Swipes." De Doe nodded. With raised eyebrows, the old man looked at the others, "Nope, never heard of him." One of the other men spoke up and said that he had been in Boxville one year before and maybe there was a man that lived there by that name but he did not personally know him. To drive the point home, Loring laid it on in his thickest Southern accent, insisting that he did indeed know a Harry Swipes in Boxville, "Y'r don't know 'im! That's your loss! He's jus' the deades' shot you ever saw. An smart with his little shootin' iron! Greased litnin's no wha? An' he's got 'er sister too! By the holy poker! Can't she sing, 'an can't she make 'er pianner howl!" Not being able to stop himself, he put the crowning touch on the whole thing. "You jes' come over tr'morrer an' I'll interduce y'r."[5] This final boast convinced the troop of Southern sympathizers that Loring and de Doe were indeed Confederate soldiers on furlough.

Tensions eased and the brothers in arms loosened up and began to socialize. They asked about Loring's leg and what was wrong with it. Cursing, Loring made up a story about how he had been shot in the knee by one of the cowardly Yankees.

One of the rebels who had now taken a liking to the fraudulent

Confederates warned them that they had best be on their way and to do so quietly. He mentioned that Captain Poole of the Home Guard was in the area looking for deserters.

Taking this advice, Loring tucked the outdated and overdue pass back in his pouch. Intent on avoiding an encounter with Captain Poole, Loring and de Doe melted into the night.[6]

14

De Doe Is Dead?!

Peering through the brush, Loring and de Doe saw that they had reached the outskirts of Boxville. Trying to avoid an encounter with Captain Poole, they skirted around the village and headed toward the Navidad River.[1] The river was dry. With their hopes of floating downriver dashed, they continued to move south along the dry riverbed toward the junction with the Lavaca River.

Reaching a small grove of trees, they found water. Here they rested and waited for the sun to settle on the horizon, then they walked until midnight. Finally they found a suitable place to spend the night and settled in as the mosquitos emerged. Not wanting to be on the damp ground, Loring hauled himself up into the crotch of an old oak tree, while de Doe flopped down on the ground, impervious to the flying tormentors. Loring dozed and dreamed of home as he watched the familiar constellations overhead. There was comfort in seeing the same stars he had seen so often from the decks of so many ships.

When Loring awoke the sun was already up. Climbing down from his perch, he poked de Doe with his boot but could not rouse him. Bending over, he gave him a gentle nudge but still could not wake his companion. "Good God is he dead? He is dead!"[2] De Doe appeared to have simply expired from exhaustion during the night. Kneeling down, Loring shook de Doe roughly before rolling him over. This could not be. De Doe, although as tired as Loring himself, had seemed fine the previous evening. How could he have been so careless as to not check on his companion during the night? Loring felt a tremendous responsibility for the care of de Doe. As the senior officer it was his duty to look after this man. How could he have let this happen? What would he do? Should he bury de Doe here and continue on? Loring had no shovel to dig a grave. No means to mark the grave. He didn't have the strength to carry de Doe and seek help at the nearest house to bury him. He couldn't just leave him here, those dogs would surely find him. Loring bent over his comrade and rolled him over onto his back. De Doe snorted. Loring put his head to de Doe's chest. He could hear a heartbeat. This man was not dead.

De Doe was still breathing but seemed to be unconscious. Loring grabbed de Doe's shoulders and shook him. De Doe sprang to his feet and shouted, "What goes there?" He appeared fully recuperated from any of the hardships that they had endured thus far. Surprised at his companion's sudden return from death's door, Loring took a step back, overjoyed that his comrade was still alive. "My god, man, I thought you had expired. You gave me a fright." De Doe, back from the dead, simply stated, "I'm hungry."

It had been three days since the men had last eaten. Around them was nothing but a vast prairie of parched, cracked dirt with a few wilted spiny weeds poking through. Following a road for several hours, they came upon a small cottage. An old gray-haired, one-eyed veteran toiled in the front yard of the house. Wasting no time, Loring asked if some food could be spared for a couple of very tired and poor Confederate soldiers. The old man squinted, his good eye focused on the men standing before him. He took a moment to look them over. Loring kept talking and relayed their recent desperate experiences. Without turning his head the old one-eyed veteran yelled over his shoulder to a woman inside the cottage to prepare some cornbread and bacon for the men.

A shriveled-up old woman emerged from the basement of the cottage. She carried some ribs on her shoulder and folded in her apron was some cornbread. The ribs looked thin and moldy, but the cornbread smelled fresh. Loring and de Doe sat in the yard and ate with the old man and his wife watching, neither saying a word.[3] After the meal, the woman cut up some additional cornbread into small chunks and placed them in an old sock. With a withered and bony old hand she gave the sock to de Doe. "Good luck to ye." Loring stood and thanked them for their kindness. The old man smiled a toothless grin. Loring and de Doe passed through the gate down the road.

Loring turned as he heard the distinctive sound of hoofbeats. De Doe looked back as well. Within half a mile of the cottage, a carriage came up behind them and drew close. A dapper man was seated next to a Negro driving the carriage. The carriage slowed down. Loring hissed at de Doe to not turn around. The driver pulled back on the reins and the carriage stopped beside the pair. Loring turned to say hello and was greeted by the well-dressed man, who produced a large revolver. Not willing to take any chances, he pointed the gun at the strangers and began to question them. "Who are you and where are you going?"[4]

It was immediately clear to Loring that this man, probably a local judge, was not to be trifled with. Loring met each question with a short, deliberate answer. He launched into his well-practiced monologue about being Confederate soldiers on furlough as de Doe nodded for emphasis. Only partially convinced but with other obviously pressing matters to attend to, the judge holstered his revolver. In a dismissive tone the judge said good day and elbowed the Negro driver in the ribs to continue on. The horse lunged at the slap of the reins and the carriage moved on, leaving a relieved Loring and de Doe to continue their trek.

The afternoon wore on. The monotony of always having to find water and the boredom of the road were exacerbated by the pain of their raw, blistered feet and sore legs. The men found themselves on the banks of the Navidad River as evening approached. With little effort they found a small rowboat along the banks of the river. Borrowing the boat, they rowed across the Navidad. On the opposite shore, they found an inn. With some trepidation they carefully approached the establishment. Knocking on the door, they were met by Mrs. Southerland, the owner of the rowboat and the proprietress of the inn.

With his hat in hand Loring asked if she might spare some food for two poor soldiers headed home on furlough. Without hesitation Mrs. Southerland, being a good Christian woman, assured them she would do just that even though it certainly appeared as though they could not pay for such. She seemed quite sympathetic to the plight of the men and explained that her son was a Confederate soldier. In fact, he was at home on furlough. She was sure that he would enjoy meeting some fellow comrades in arms. She would be sure to introduce them. Hearing this, de Doe was unable to control himself and yelled out, "Great Napoleon!," as if they had just walked into a hotbed of snakes. Loring cast a scornful glance at de Doe's outburst.

Mrs. Southerland made the introductions and the three soldiers quickly became friendly. Over the next several hours, they swapped stories of heroic battles and cursed the Yankees. Loring went so far as to tell the tale of the battle of Calcasieu Pass. Speaking from the Southern perspective, he provided details of the actual battle, which were obviously quite convincing. Mrs. Southerland's son sat up. Loring stared. The Confederate mentioned that he had heard of that battle. In fact, he recalled that one of the ships surrendered almost immediately but the other fought like hell. It was led by a Captain Lory or some such name. De Doe squirmed. Loring finished the story and changed the topic. During the after-dinner conversation, Loring learned that there was a steamer bound for Matagorda and it was moored only nine miles away in Texana.[5]

With dinner over and pleasantries exchanged, Loring and de Doe thanked their hosts and borrowed the little rowboat once more. As they drifted downriver toward Texana and the waiting steamer, Loring thought that perhaps their luck had changed. If they could book passage on the steamer to Matagorda Bay they could avoid fifty miles of walking and freedom would be so much closer at hand.

15

The Hunter

The Navidad River was beginning to fill the bottom of the rowboat.[1] The men were in danger of being swamped, and de Doe was again in a very precarious situation, as his ability to swim was marginal at best. Luckily the river was so shallow it barely provided the few inches of water necessary to keep the small craft afloat.

As the river entered a forest the men encountered various trees that had fallen across the channel, obstructing their progress. They hauled the boat over debris caught in the twisted branches of the trees and slid it under thick trunks lying across the river. The amount of effort it took to move the boat around the downed trees was taking its toll on the weary men. The water inside the leaking boat was now deeper than the river itself. The precious stock of cornbread had tumbled off the bench seat and was floating alongside various items of clothing in the muddy water in the bottom of the boat. After two hours of hauling the boat over and under the maze of obstacles and having made only a half mile of progress, they abandoned it. Wet, exhausted, sore, and hungry, Loring and de Doe climbed up onto the riverbank and laid in the dew of the grass as the cold crept into their bones. As the sun slipped below the horizon, the mosquitoes emerged to stalk and torment the two wanderers.

The night was the same as so many previously spent, swatting swarms of mosquitos while huddling together to try and stay warm. The men welcomed the warmth of the morning sun as it dried their clothing, and they lolled about until sleep overcame them. Around noon they awoke. Loring stood up and noticed that his hip and leg felt stronger and seemed to be partially recovered. His spirit was buoyed at the thought of making better progress throughout the day.

The men set off through the woods, being careful to stay out of sight. After several hours of tramping on the banks of the Navidad River they came to a junction where the Navidad emptied into the Lavaca River.[2]

From the brushy banks of the junction with the Lavaca River they scanned the opposite shore and could see a slightly larger boat than the one borrowed from Mrs. Southerland. De Doe was relieved to see that there was a bridge across the river and he would not have to attempt to swim across to reach the boat. They would wait until dark before attempting to cross the bridge to borrow this fine vessel. Once they had liberated the boat they would then row the thirty miles down the Lavaca River to Matagorda Bay and not have to chance the passage on the steamer in Texana.

After dark the pair crossed the bridge over the Lavaca River and crept into the small town of Texana in search of some victuals. Not wanting to arouse any suspicion, Loring approached a slave standing on a corner and asked for the nearest source of bread. The response was that there was no bakery in town but they might be able to ask for some bread at a nearby house.

The pangs of hunger could no longer be ignored. Loring realized he needed to use a couple of the gold coins that he had kept hidden in order to buy some food. He had sewn these gold coins into the band of his trousers on the second day of his imprisonment in Camp Groce. He had carried them with him ever since and had never mentioned to anyone that he had them. These same coins had been in his waist belt when the Confederate provost marshal Captain McDade assembled roll call for the first time at Camp Groce. As an honorable officer, Loring was expected to empty his pockets of everything and he would not be subjected to a personal search. He had handed over some greenbacks and a gold pocket watch during the assembly but kept the gold coins and his small penknife, with no one ever being the wiser. Now the actual value of the coins had become greater than their sentimental value and one or two of the coins would have to be sacrificed to purchase some food if any could be found.

It was difficult to ignore the pangs of hunger, but Loring thought twice. The potential for disaster outweighed the need for the few bites of cornbread they sought. Forgoing a possible meal in order to maintain their freedom, they made their way along the riverbank to the place where they had seen the rowboat earlier in the day. As they coasted through the tall grass along the river, they spied a couple of even larger boats, about seventeen feet in length, pulled up on shore. Then a voice drifted toward them, followed by the unmistakable sound of oars dipping in the water.

Keeping close to the water's edge and hunkering down in the thick undergrowth, Loring and de Doe hid and watched the river traffic. A scow floated past and pulled into shore. A man got out and walked up the bank about two hundred feet away from them. With no time to waste, Loring kept low and scrambled sixty yards to the boat. He quickly scanned the interior for food or any other items that might be useful. Finding nothing to eat and nothing useful but an old tin cup, he pushed the boat into the water. Loring grabbed an oar, placed it in the oarlock, and scanned the bottom of the boat for the second oar. There was none. The owner had simply used the one oar as a paddle.[3]

Removing the oar from the lock, Loring moved to the bow of the boat. Perched in the bow, Loring took two strokes on one side and then two on the other. Raising the oar vertically from the water after each stroke, he was careful to make as little noise as possible.

To avoid detection, Loring paddled directly across the river to where they had originally started. Seeing this, de Doe recrossed the bridge and watched from the brush for any oncoming boat traffic. As Loring neared the shore, de Doe gave a barely audible whistle to let Loring know he was in the right spot. When Loring slid the boat close to shore, de Doe wasted no time. He grabbed the bow and in one motion gave a mighty push, propelling them out into the middle of the river as he jumped onboard. Even under the cover of darkness the men were completely exposed in the middle of the river. Loring decided it was best to try and blend in and hide in plain sight. Drifting downriver, the pair struck up a merry banter as they broke into song and pretended to be locals.[4]

Loring paddled past various boats and ships filled with Confederate soldiers, sailors, and Southerners. Their banter and songs drew laughter and retorts from the rebel crews as they paddled on unmolested down the Lavaca River. Once they were beyond a bend in the river and away from the majority of larger ships and crews, Loring and de Doe searched the boat once more. They found some fishing line, pieces of boards, and a large folding knife. Using the large knife, they split the one good oar in half lengthwise, creating two.

With this second oar, de Doe joined Loring on the same seat and they began to pull down river. They rowed the rest of the night and all through the next day. Still having not eaten any substantial meal in over three days, their hunger pains were now dulled by a thirst that grew in intensity as the sun climbed higher in the sky. The men had traveled far enough south that they were in the tidal flats—the river water was brackish, salty, and not fit to drink. They had to find some fresh water soon. As they continued still farther downriver the water slowed and several channels opened up. Deciding to follow the strongest current, Loring and de Doe drifted into the delta toward Matagorda Bay. The heat had become oppressive, and the men had not had anything to drink in over twelve hours.[5] Deciding to move toward shore and search for water, they pulled up on a sandy point.

Stepping out of the boat and crawling up the sandy bank, the two men rolled onto their backs to rest. Loring heard some rustling in the dry brush just beyond the point as someone approached. Just as Loring and de Doe sprang to their feet, a man dressed in drab clothing appeared on the sandy point! Suspicious, he questioned Loring. "Did you see a large sailboat up the river?"[6] Loring told him that they had indeed seen a large boat a few miles below Texana. Loring then asked if there was any fresh water in the vicinity. The man pointed and explained that nearby was the remains of a plantation that had burned down about four years earlier. The cistern would surely still have plenty of water in it. Noticing that the wind was beginning to pick up, the man suggested they leave soon or it might become too strong and rough for them to row around the point.

Taking the suggestion and wanting to put some distance between them and this unknown man, Loring and de Doe climbed back into the rowboat and shoved off.

Pulling out into the water, they made some headway. But as soon as they rounded the point the full force of the wind hit them.

The water became choppy and the men had to put their backs into it just to keep from being blown sideways. As they strained against the wind the oars began to bend from the pressure. The boat bobbed up and down in the swells as the waves broke over the bow. To continue any farther would court disaster. They rowed to shore and pulled the boat up on the sand, still a half mile away from the cistern.

Now on foot, Loring and de Doe stumbled toward the former plantation. Finally reaching it, they quickly found the cistern. Peering into its depths, they "looked down upon the water's ravishing face—several feet below."[7] How cruel, the water so close and yet so far. Rummaging about in the wreckage of the home, they found an old nail keg but no rope with which to lower it into the water. Remembering the fishing line in the boat, Loring staggered the half mile back to the boat to retrieve it. The mile round trip was punishing for Loring, who crawled the final one hundred yards to the well. Twisting and doubling the fishing line upon itself, they made a braid strong enough to hoist the water-filled keg to the surface. They dropped the keg down into the well and hauled it back up to yield a half pint of water.

As Loring and de Doe quenched their thirst, the suspicious man who had given them directions to the cistern reappeared from the brush. Only now, he was holding a double-barreled shotgun used for upland game or waterfowl hunting.[8] He questioned Loring and de Doe again. Wary, Loring provided only vague answers to the man's questions. Seemingly satisfied, the man offered them passage farther downriver to the open bay. De Doe was ready to accept, but Loring was suspicious and thought this man was a little too eager and interested in them. The hunter abruptly turned around and left.

Loring and de Doe decided to rest before continuing. Finding an old wagon shed nearby, de Doe crawled in and fell fast asleep. Loring searched the immediate vicinity for anything that they might use to strengthen their boat and repair the flimsy makeshift oars. Finding nothing of use, he too crawled inside the shed and laid down but could not sleep.

As Loring settled in, distant voices could be heard a few hundred yards away, just over a rise. Loring came to attention, his senses fully alert. He peeked out of the shed through a crack in the boards. He could see the tips of three bayonets glinting in the sun.[9] In a hoarse, urgent voice Loring whispered to de Doe, "Wake up!"

At 150 yards, the soldiers' gun barrels became clearly visible. Cresting the rise were three soldiers and a sergeant, fifty yards away. The Confederate soldiers could see the shed and its occupants. The rebel sergeant "commanded—with a slight veneer of politeness, Surrender, gentlemen, and give up your arms."[10] De Doe, now fully awake himself, stared in disbelief.

Loring called out to the approaching soldiers, "What do you mean by this nonsense? You must be joking. We are soldiers like yourselves only unarmed, being on furlough. You better go home if you have any: if not, go and fight your battles on some other field."[11]

The rebel soldiers were not deterred. With muskets leveled at the shed and moving toward the cornered men, the Confederate sergeant again called out for Loring and de Doe to surrender.

With nowhere to run, Loring and de Doe put their hands up and stepped out of the shed. Loring again protested. De Doe chimed in. The sergeant was undeterred. At bayonet point Loring and de Doe were marched back to the beach where their rowboat rested on the sand. A larger skiff was waiting with six Confederate soldiers. One of the rebel soldiers made an offhand comment to one of his compatriots that no one had set foot on the point by the old plantation for over a year. The hunter stood nearby speaking with one of the men and pointed as Loring and de Doe came into sight. Forcing the two men into the skiff, the sergeant explained they would be taken back to Lavaca to be interrogated by the provost marshal.[12]

It was surreal, it had happened so quickly. How could this be? They were so close to making it to Union lines and freedom. De Doe was stunned and didn't say anything. Loring was shocked at first. His shock turned to anger and then to steadfast resolve. It was clear to Loring that the suspicious hunter had turned them in as deserters. Loring and de Doe had traveled over two hundred miles in ten days, only to be recaptured just a few miles from Matagorda and a ship to freedom.

16

Interrogation

Loring and de Doe quietly sat side by side on a long bench in the skiff. Their hands were tied behind their backs. The boat ride was brief. The skiff pulled up along a muddy bank after being rowed only a mile back upriver. Both men were helped to their feet after they fell out of the boat on the landing. The long walk back to Lavaca, under guard, was painful physically and nearly debilitating mentally. Loring kept thinking about how to play the next hand that might be dealt them in discussions with their interrogator. De Doe could not help but play the events over and over in his mind, wondering how this could be happening and what would become of them. Reaching the port of Lavaca, the men were placed under guard and told to wait for the provost marshal, who would interrogate them.[1]

The guards snapped to attention as the provost marshal entered the room. He sat down and stared at Loring and de Doe, sizing them up. He looked over the official report of their capture and then matter of factly asked the two men who they were and what they were doing out on the point. Very calmly Loring launched into his practiced story of how they were Confederate artillerymen who had been onboard the tinclad gunboat *J. F. Carr* and were heading home on furlough.[2] The provost marshal smirked at hearing this. He knew that the captain of the *J. F. Carr* would be arriving at the port soon, and then he would have immutable proof one way or the other whether this was true or not. Loring quickly noted that the provost marshal was intellectually much more capable than the Confederates and Southern sympathizers they had previously encountered. Loring's story of two Confederate artillerymen on furlough would be unlikely to stand up under scrutiny.

The provost marshal continued the interrogation, asking the men about the geography of the area. Loring again answered for both men, but his knowledge of the area was limited to the contraband maps smuggled into the prison. De Doe had no such knowledge and so could contribute nothing. The provost marshal was not fooled in the least. He was intimately familiar with Lavaca, Boxville, and the surrounding area. As Loring spun his story, the provost marshal sat and listened. Seemingly amused, he sat back and clasped his hands behind his head. Loring continued, but based on his interrogator's body language he was now sure his story would soon fall "apart as a rope of sand."[3]

The provost marshal motioned for Loring to conclude his story. He abruptly pushed himself away from the desk and stood up. As he walked toward the door he sternly told the guards, "Lock them up." Loring and de Doe were placed in irons and roughly led away. Yet as bad a situation as this was, there was a silver lining to being locked up, at least for the moment: supper! The two men were given what amounted to a feast: "cornbread, bacon and corn coffee."[4] With bellies full, the two suspected Confederate deserters lay down indoors, with no mosquitos to torment them, and slept. As Loring drifted off he estimated he had slept a total of ten hours in the last ten days.

The next morning the provost marshal again summoned the suspected deserters and asked them a few questions. Without hesitation and after only a moment of consideration he delivered his verdict, explaining that he did not believe they were Confederate soldiers. Nor did he think they were Southerners. Based on the facts delivered in their story and the papers they had presented, they did not appear to have served on the gunboat *J. F. Carr*. They didn't even know the captain's name. They had not fooled him by their dress, the way in which they carried themselves, or their mannerisms. It was clear to him that they were escaped Federals fleeing the country. Calling them counterfeit Confederates, he added, "If you are, you may as well say so, for you will be much better treated than you will be as deserters."[5]

Loring carefully considered that last statement. De Doe swallowed hard. The provost marshal stood up. The stern look on his face made it clear he was out of patience. While Loring considered his next words very carefully, the provost marshal added that Captain Brown of the *J. F. Carr* was expected to arrive the next day. The captain would settle the matter of whether or not the two were legitimate. If they were indeed Confederates, Loring and de

Doe would accompany the captain back to the ship, where their sentence as deserters would be carried out and they would likely be hanged. If they were not Confederates . . . well, then, that decision was yet to be made.

In his best Southern drawl Loring stubbornly made a final attempt to dissuade the provost marshal from presenting them for inspection to the captain. The provost marshal slammed his fist down on the desk hard enough to make the nearest guard jump. That was all, no further rebuff could persuade him from having the captain of the *J. F. Carr* decide the issue. The provost marshal's posturing and demeanor made it clear that the ruse was over.

Loring drew himself up and stood at attention; de Doe followed suit. In his native New England accent, Loring declared, "We are United States Naval Officers; escaped prisoners from Camp Groce."[6] With this confession the provost marshal's demeanor softened. His relief showed, as his shoulders dropped and the tension in his face eased. "Well, then, gentlemen, as officers you must dine with me this evening," he said. De Doe was confused and looked at Loring. Loring looked the provost marshal in the eye and said, "Of course, sir, if you insist."

That evening Loring and de Doe joined the provost marshal and his staff for dinner. The same three soldiers who had captured Loring and de Doe were still guarding them and had not slept in two days. With no other relief available for the guards, the provost marshal decided he would personally provide relief and guard the prisoners. Deciding to make a bit of a party out of the situation, the provost marshal invited his staff and a few friends to share guard duty. The captives and captors dined and played euchre well into the night.

The next day Captain Brown of the *J. F. Carr* arrived and confidently declared that the prisoners were not members of his crew. The provost marshal ordered the prisoners back to Camp Groce. Facing an uncertain future, Loring and de Doe knew the only thing they could count on would be the wrath of Colonel Gillespie.

17

A Night Drive

Loring and de Doe were escorted onboard a schooner anchored in Lavaca Bay for the first part of the journey back to Camp Groce. The ship was soon under way toward Indianola and then to Matagorda Bay.[1] As the schooner passed Indianola, the damage from the Union shelling back in 1862 was still clearly visible from the ship's deck. The destruction was devastating. Loring was reminded of what deadly business they were all engaged in. He needed to get back in the fight. He and de Doe had been so close to freedom. Carelessness. That was it. He should have listened to his gut. He should have insisted that they move on after drinking their fill from the well at the burned-out plantation. Now who knew what waited for them. At midnight the ship anchored just off Matagorda. Loring and de Doe were handcuffed together to prevent any shenanigans.

At midmorning the forlorn pair were rowed ashore and placed in the custody of a Confederate officer. Still dressed in their ragged Confederate uniforms, Loring and de Doe were provided with a change of clothing, which included shirts, pants, and a pair of proper shoes for de Doe, who was still wearing the moccasins Loring had made for him.

The officer in charge decided that the best way to proceed with transporting the prisoners was by wagon forty miles. They would follow the Colorado River for thirty miles north, then head due east to Columbia, and then travel by rail to Houston. Loring and de Doe would be guarded by a heavily armed Confederate by the name of Jones and a teamster of German descent. At ten that evening the prisoners boarded a "covered democrat wagon drawn by a pair of little-dog mules and set out for a prospective lonely night ride."[2] Ready for a long ride, Loring was eager to be as comfortable as possible. He struck a deal with Jones that if he would remove their handcuffs they promised not to escape.

Jones seemed a rather happy fellow, aided by an ever-present bottle of rum. Through the night Loring attempted to enjoy the constant conversation provided by this jolly fellow, but his enjoyment was tempered by the road itself.

The road had recently been cut through a forest and was nothing more than a rough path with tree stumps sticking up everywhere. The driver tried to weave in and out to avoid the stumps but was not doing a very good job, at least according to Jones. In his half-inebriated state Jones felt that he could drive the wagon far better than the German holding the reins. Convincing the German to switch with him, Jones took the reins and led them on a ride they would not soon forget.

The stumps of the recently cut trees were about a foot high. In the dark and drunk, Jones made no attempt to maneuver the mule team around the stumps, despite the declarations of Loring, de Doe, and the German. Jones shouted at his passengers that he did not mind the rough road, nor should they. With feet braced against the sides of the wagon, the passengers grabbed their seats and clenched their teeth as the wagon rolled over the waves of stumps. The mules stumbled and lurched, causing the wagon to buck and bounce. The wheels rolled over stumps completely or partially and slipped off sideways. The axles would at times catch the tops and be lifted up, only to slam back down. Twice Jones himself was tossed out of the wagon head over heel. Both times, as the wagon slammed down the buckboard springs compressed and then released, catapulting Jones head first over the side. De Doe looked at Loring, eyebrows raised. Loring peered over the side of the wagon, thinking perhaps Jones might be dazed and they could simply wander off. They had no such luck. Amazingly uninjured, Jones climbed back aboard the wagon each time and continued on. After two hours of pitching to and fro among the swell of stumps the small wagon pulled away from the former forest onto the flat prairie. Jones thankfully drew in the reins and they stopped for a while to feed and rest the mules. With the new day dawning Jones handed the reins back to the German and declared, "There, I got us through the rough part." They resumed the journey toward Columbia.[3]

Reaching the outskirts of Columbia around 11:00 a.m., Loring and de Doe were clapped in irons.[4] As they were turned over to the local military authorities, it was made clear that although they were not in uniform these men were Union officers. As such they were to be treated with the respect befitting their rank. Loring and de Doe dined with the Confederate officers that evening.

Columbia seemed to have been overlooked by the destruction of war. There were signs of a thriving trade; businesses were open and a steady stream of customers moved in and out of the stores. The wharf along the Brazos River was lined with various types of blockade-running ships being fitted and loaded to make the dash to the sea. Here in this untouched corner of the war Loring and de Doe enjoyed a real luxury, coffee. In this case it was a "cup of Lincoln Coffee par excellence in distinction to its rival beverage, the Davis corn article."[5] The luxury abruptly ended the following morning. The two men were herded aboard rail cars for the seven-hour trip to Houston. They were thrown on a flat car among many slaves being transported to work the fields or be sold. The men sat down on the sparse straw strewn across the wood floor. As they looked about the car they were met with far-off stares from people who had simply accepted that they were a commodity being shipped to the next point of use. Not a word was exchanged. It was a stark reminder of what they were fighting for. It reaffirmed for Loring that this war was not just about his freedom but that of an entire race. He had to get back into the fight, he had to escape and report for duty.

18

A Confederate Bastille

rriving in Houston, Loring and de Doe were hastily dealt with. The provost marshal waved his hand and dismissed them, stating, "Away with them to the courthouse!"[1] Loring looked at de Doe and smiled. Courthouses were generally regal buildings. It would provide some small amount of justice, or in this case more comfortable quarters than the pair had seen the past ten days. At the very least they would be inside.

Loring's optimism did not last long. Marching up the steps to the courthouse, they discovered that the majestic structure had been denigrated in order to house as many prisoners as its walls could envelop. The former "temple of justice" had been retrofitted with iron bars and massive bolts to create a labyrinth of cells crammed full of all sorts of miscreants, both military and civilian. Loring and de Doe were shoved into a cell that stunk of prison filth. It seemed to Loring that this was a "Confederate Bastille."[2]

Crowded among common criminals, political prisoners, and those who simply dissented from the Confederate position, Loring and de Doe quickly discovered some of the darkest secrets of the rebel prisons. To their surprise they found themselves incarcerated with the *Wave*'s former pilot.

The pilot had been in the prison for some time. He had been tried for treason and then held to be tried once more. For weeks he had been shackled with ball and chain. Speaking further with the pilot, Loring learned that other members of the *Wave*'s crew had also been imprisoned in the courthouse.

There was no lengthy reunion. After a brief stay in the bastille Loring and de Doe were again herded aboard a train, headed directly to Camp Groce and an uncertain encounter with Colonel Gillespie. Three hours later the pair stood outside the gates of Camp Groce, gravely concerned about what fate awaited them on their return.

They did not have to wait long. Colonel Gillespie strode into sight. In a voice full of bravado, he boomed, "You can't get away from me! I can catch you every time! I will make it hot for you."[3] He kept his word. Loring and de Doe were not permitted to step inside the gates of the camp. They had no contact with their incarcerated comrades. They were each given a thin blanket, turned about, and marched back to the train. They boarded an open car and were sent to the Anderson Grimes County Jail, to be held indefinitely.

The night of July 21 the two men arrived in Navasota, Texas, and the gates of the Anderson Grimes County Jail. Guards with bayonets fixed to their muskets prodded the men forward. As the huge iron doors clanged shut behind them Loring and de Doe sank to the floor. Loring gave de Doe a reassuring nod. As Loring closed his eyes he was sure of only one thing: whatever misfortune the next day would bring, he would endure it.

19

Anderson Grimes County Jail

Loring awoke early. Committed to surveying his surroundings, he immediately began to talk with the other inmates. Loring did a double take; he was surprised to see a familiar face. Rogers?![1] Loring thought that Rogers had lost his nerve the night of July 4 and that was why he had not been at the rendezvous point in Camp Groce. Rogers was just as surprised to see Loring. The men sat down on the filthy floor and Rogers explained to Loring what had happened the night of the escape and how he was captured.

Rogers arrived at the rendezvous point and, seeing no one else there, determined he must be late. He decided to move on alone and crawled through the wall at a different point. Not having the skill to navigate at night, he wandered about in circles. As day broke he was only four miles from the prison. He pushed on, but by the second day the bloodhounds cut his tracks. He was hunted down and recaptured.

Rogers's return to Camp Groce was short-lived. Colonel Gillespie met him at the gate of the prison but would not let him enter. Rogers was provided with a blanket and sent to the Anderson Grimes County Jail. To add to his misery, Rogers had been forced to wear a ball and chain for weeks. Continuing, Rogers explained that the county jail had been converted to house the worst criminals in the area inside its overcrowded, putrid walls.

As Rogers finished his story, Confederate captain Webb stepped up to the cell. He motioned for Loring. The captain opened the cell and told him to step out. Loring was to be moved to the dungeon, where he would be held and required to wear a ball and chain. Loring vehemently began to argue against this. "I am not a criminal, I have broken no laws, and I am not a slave!" None but a cowardly soldier devoid of gentlemanly instinct would inflict such disgraceful abuse upon a prisoner of war. "Were you in my place would you allow such brutality to be served upon you without an argument?"

Captain Webb began to respond but stopped short and took a step back. Loring's words struck a chord with him. Webb decided he would ponder this further and take it up with General Magruder, the commanding officer. Webb told Loring he would not be required to wear a ball and chain until General Magruder had the opportunity to consider the issue, as long as Loring promised to not escape. Loring agreed, at least until the matter had been settled.

The Anderson Grimes County Jail was a two-story stone structure surrounded by a twelve-foot-high wooden fence. Two sentry boxes sat on the corners of the fence, diagonal from each other. The building itself contained two large rooms, one upper and one lower. The building's enormous gates were secured with a seventy-five pound lock and two enormous iron crossbars.[2] The structure was built like a fortress meant to keep people out, rather than keeping prisoners inside. A small hole, about a foot square, provided the only light and air to the upper floor. This area was accessed from the outside via a narrow door leading to an exterior flight of stairs, which was nearly vertical to prevent a large number of people from ascending at one time.

Loring was locked away in the upper room. There were few creature comforts: a cot, a couple of chairs, and two tables. One of the tables had a crude checkerboard carved into the top.

Loring acclimated and became acquainted with several of the residents. Mr. Gildart, who held treasonous opinions, was among these characters.[3] He was a rather articulate fellow and would climb on top of the large table and espouse his blasphemous Union views in a fiery tongue. Dr. Peebles was a local physician and suspected Northern sympathizer. With known enemies on the outside, Peebles had been the target of a local mob that had attempted to storm the prison. Only the arrival of a squad of soldiers from Camp Groce combined with the difficulty of navigating the narrow, nearly vertical stairs leading to the upper floor and the massive padlock saved the doctor from his "friends" and a noose around his neck.

Also imprisoned was a Confederate soldier by the name of Rose. As a guard on the railroad, he had been involved in an incident in which a rebel soldier had been killed. Rose was charged with the murder. The dead man's friends had tracked Rose down. The unruly mob stormed the prison to try and administer their own justice but were foiled by the massive padlock. Unwilling to give up, the mob attempted to poison Rose. Through the heavily barred hole they passed Rose a bottle of whiskey that had been compromised. The bottle was a token of their supposed good will. Rose took one sip of the whiskey and spit it out. Another inmate grabbed the whiskey from Rose. Not wanting it to go to waste, he drained half the bottle before Rose could say a word. Within two hours the poor wretch writhed in agony on the floor and died.

The prison did not discriminate. Incarcerated with the others was a slave by the name of Jolly Jeff who had a habit of running away from his master. He had been caught by bounty hunters and was relegated to the prison until he could be claimed by his owner. He was constantly at Rose's side, making fun, singing, jumping about, and providing entertainment for the others.

Despite the companionship of these characters the conditions in the jail were horrific, with dozens of men crammed into the upper and lower floors of the jail. Men slept on the floor with perhaps only a thin blanket to keep them warm. Buckets used as toilets were emptied once a day, and rations were minimal. Death from starvation was prolonged due to the kindness and charity of two women, Mrs. Cone and Mrs. Wilson.[4] Several times a week these Christian ladies had a slave deliver buttermilk, okra, and bread to the prisoners. Mrs. Cone's husband, the recently elected sheriff of Grimes County, often accompanied his wife to the jail.[5] He would ascend the stairs to the second floor to visit with Rose, a family friend. After only a few days in the Anderson Grimes County Jail Loring realized that it was not intended to be a place of long-term incarceration; it was a place of final interment. Knowing that he could not last long in such a place, he began to plan an escape.

Within three days Loring had a plan; however, he had promised to not escape until the matter of the ball and chain had been addressed. A man of his word, Loring felt it would be best to expedite that matter and then get on with the escape. He made it a point to inquire with Captain Webb regarding the decision. Webb explained that he had received no word from General Magruder.[6] In the absence of any guidance on the issue Webb decided to forgo having Loring clapped in irons with ball and chain. He would also see to it that Loring and de Doe were both moved from the upper floor to the dungeon. While conditions inside the lower floor, or dungeon, were worse than those on the upper floor, the men were at least allowed outside in the yard during the day, a small consolation. But as dusk fell the men would be required to return to the dungeon.

Within two weeks the lack of food and proper hygiene took its toll on the men. Loring's, de Doe's, and Rogers's health began to fail. Loring appealed to Captain Webb regarding the meager rations. But his pleas fell on deaf ears. Webb justified the rations as the same as those provided to the Confederate soldiers. Loring knew the treatment was intentional; he had seen with his own eyes the large herds of cattle grazing on the prairie. There was ample food for the right people.

Hunger pains fueled discussion of escape. Among the military prisoners housed in the jail, loyalty to the Union cause began to wane. On August 8 the men in blue were given a stark reminder of what they had been fighting for.

At midmorning several heavily armed guards entered the yard as Loring watched from a corner. Following the guards was a Southern gentleman. Three of the guards climbed the stairs to the upper floor. Some scuffling and cussing could be heard. Out of the upper door emerged a guard followed by Jolly Jeff and the remaining guards. Once on the ground, the gentlemen slapped irons around the wrists of the slave. A heavy ox chain was looped around Jeff's neck and tightened until the veins bulged on his forehead.[7] A ten-foot leather strap with a clasp on the end was then attached to the ox chain, as if Jeff were a dog on a leash. The Southern gentleman yanked down on the leather strap, nearly knocking Jeff off his feet. Gasping and grabbing with shackled hands at the leather strap, Jeff was led out of the yard. Loring took a step forward. One of the guards leveled his bayonet-tipped musket at him and shook his head in a menacing manner. There was nothing Loring could do. The Southern man never looked back at Jeff or spoke to him. Bent half over and with solemn eyes, Jeff glanced sideways at Loring as he was led through the yard. By the time Jeff reached the gate word had spread that this was Jeff's master coming to claim his property. The image of this man, shackled and leashed, being led back into bondage was forever burned into Loring's brain.

As the men's physical health declined so did their mental health. The boredom and monotony of imprisonment ate away at them. Day after day of nothing, the hot days, the cold nights, no food, wretched conditions, no word of exchange, and constant abuse by some of the guards caused some men to lose any hope of ever leaving alive. Weeks stretched to over a month and still the same monotonous routine of nothing. The men's bodies showed signs of malnutrition. They had no energy, felt tired all the time, had difficulty concentrating, and became combative with each other. Loring worked hard to remain optimistic. He spent his days looking after de Doe, feeling a tremendous sense of responsibility for this young man. At night Loring would think of his family and plan his escape.

Loring knew he had to get out of this prison or he would not survive. As resilient as de Doe had been on the outside during the escape attempt, he too became despondent as his body failed. He said to those who inquired that he was tired and that he was sure he would not see many more days. His health declined to the point where he could no longer walk or stand on his own. Convinced he would not live much longer, de Doe wrote his own obituary.[8]

On August 21 Loring received a letter from Confederate captain Mason, stationed at Camp Groce. The letter informed Loring that ten of his men had died in the month since Loring had been recaptured. Camp Groce was experiencing overcrowded conditions, close confinement, a lack of food, and rampant disease. Two days later six hundred ragged Union soldiers from Camp Tyler marched past the small window at the Anderson Grimes County Jail on their way to confinement at Camp Groce.[9]

On September 6 Loring heard a rumor that the military men at the jail were going to be sent back to Camp Groce. The men waited with anticipation for the orders to be ready to vacate. A corporal made the announcement and ordered the men to be prepared to leave in thirty minutes.[10] There was some level of joy. At least they had lived long enough to see that day. For six weeks Loring and de

Doe had endured hell on earth in the Anderson Grimes County Jail. For many men it became their last resting place.

Heavily armed with revolvers, shotguns, and muskets, a guard consisting of two lieutenants, a sergeant, and three privates kept a watchful eye on Loring, de Doe, and Rogers as they were loaded onto a wagon for the trip to the Navasota Railroad.

At the depot Loring and Rogers helped carry the frail de Doe to the train. As they carefully lifted de Doe aboard the cars Loring noticed that the guards were checking passes. Moving close to a guard, he was able to briefly glance at one of the passes. As the train lurched forward Loring wished to himself for a magic pass that would allow him and his comrades to pass through the gates of the prison to freedom.

1. Gold coins carried cross-country from
California by Loring in his waist belt.

NAVY DEPARTMENT,

February 6th 1862

Sir:

You are hereby appointed an acting ___Master___

___ in the Navy of the United States, on temporary service.

After having executed the enclosed oath, and returned it to the Department, with your letter of acceptance, you will proceed without delay to Mystic Ct and report to Commander A Taylor

for duty on board iron clad Steamer under his Command

I am, respectfully,

Your obedient servant,

Gideon Welles

Secretary of the Navy.

Acting Master

Benj. W. Loring

U. S. Navy,

Washington D C.

— Detail —

2. Loring's mustering-in papers with the rank of acting master, dated February 6, 1862.

Forwarded

J. Dahlgren
Rear admiral

Forwarded by
Edm. R. Colhoun
Comdr.

July 13. 1863.

Navy Department.
29ᵗʰ June 1863.

Sir,

Having been officially mentioned for gallant conduct in action, you are hereby promoted to the grade of acting Volunteer Lieutenant in the Navy of the United States on temporary service.

Report to Rear Admiral DuPont for such duty as he may assign you.

Very Respectfully

Gideon Welles
Secretary of the Navy.

Acting Volunteer Lieutenant.
Benjamin W. Loring, U.S.N.
U.S.S. Weehawken
Port Royal S.C.

F. A. DuPont.

3. Loring's promotion to lieutenant for gallant
conduct in action on June 29, 1863.

U. S. S. "Pensacola"
Off New Orleans
March 22nd 1864

Sir:

You are hereby detached from the Command of the U.S.S. "Carrabasset" No. 49 – and will assume command of the U.S.S. Wave. No. 45.

Respectfully
Jas. S. Palmer
Commodant

To
Actg. Vol. Lieut.
Benj. F. Loring USN
Comdg. USS "Carrabasset"
No. 49.

4. Orders to Loring to take command of the tinclad uss *Wave*, dated March 22, 1864.

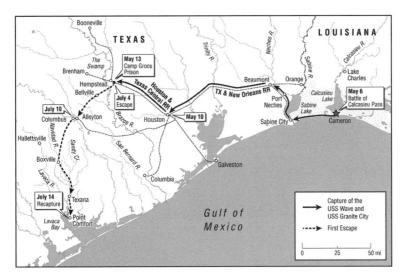

5. Map of the capture of the USS *Wave* and *Granite City* and the escape route from Camp Groce. Courtesy of the author.

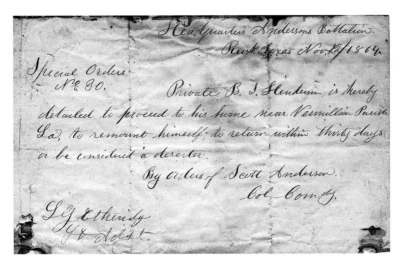

6. The forged pass that Loring used for the second escape.

7. Loring's handwritten escape map and
notes made during his second escape.

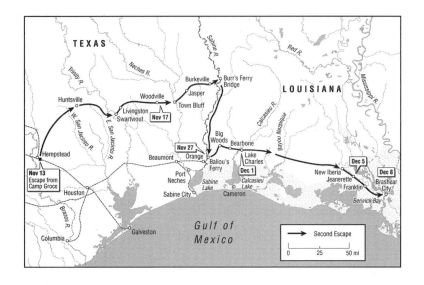

8. Map of the escape route taken by
Loring and Flory from Camp Groce.
Courtesy of the author.

9–10. Flory (*above*) and Loring (*opposite*) dressed in their Confederate escape clothes. This photo was taken after the men safely arrived in New Orleans. Note Loring's homemade moccasins.

U. S. Naval Headquarters,
No. 148 CANAL STREET.

New Orleans, La., Dec. 9, 1864.

Sir,

As you have succeeded in making your escape from the rebel authorities in Texas, and are physically debilitated and without clothes, you have permission to go North in the supply steamer Bermuda.

On your arrival at a Northern port you will report to the Department by letter, enclosing a copy of this communication, and await further orders.

Very Respectfully,

J. Palmer

Commodore.
Comdg. W.G.B.S.

Actg. Vol. Lieut.
Benj. W. Loring,
New Orleans, La.
formerly of the U.S.S. Wave.

11. Letter acknowledging Loring's escape from
Camp Groce and the toll it had taken on his health.

Forwarded by J.B. Montgomery

Navy Department,

Bureau of Equipment and Recruiting.

Washington, 12 April 1865

Sir,

Your remittance of Eight Hundred and Eighty Dollars, being deserters money, has been received and deposited by the Bureau in the Treasury.

Very Respectfully
Your Obed'& Serv't,
A. N. Smith
Chief of Bureau

A. Vol. Lieut.
R. W. Loring
Comdg. Naval Rendervous
Navy Yard
Washington D.C.

12. Letter from the Navy Department dated April 12, 1865, placing Loring at the Washington Navy Yard two days before the Lincoln assassination.

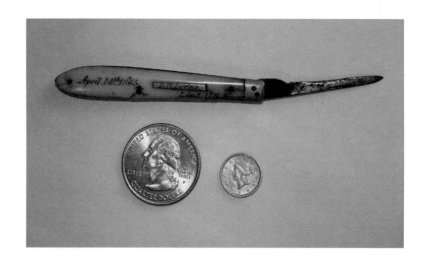

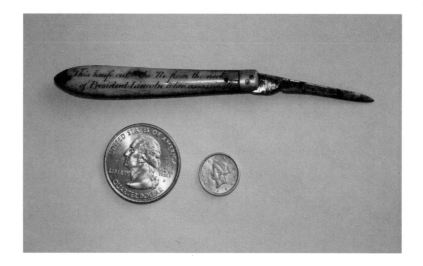

13–14. Two views of Loring's penknife, given
to him by his sister Lillie and carried with him
throughout the war. Loring used the knife to
cut the necktie from President Lincoln's neck in
Ford's Theatre the night of the assassination.

15. Loring's navy frock coat worn the night of April 14, 1865, at Ford's Theatre. Lincoln's blood is alleged to be on the coat. Courtesy of the Tioga County Historical Society, Owego, New York.

16. Loring's grave in Evergreen Cemetery, Owego, New York. Courtesy of the author.

17. A post–Civil War portrait
of Benjamin W. Loring.

20

The Old Pen Again

Loring and Rogers lifted de Doe off the train. Supporting de Doe between them, they limped toward the gates of Camp Groce. Moving through the prison gates, the stench of human effluent made them gasp. The inside of the prison was unrecognizable. Gaunt men clothed in filthy rags shuffled about the yard. Those who were too sick to leave their shed could be heard coughing and hacking. Six hundred men from Camp Tyler had been added to the already crowded enclosure, further straining the minimal resources available to properly care for the prisoners.

With the war dragging on into its fourth year, the South's resources were severely strained. Everything was rationed: food, clothing, and personnel. The German guards who had so eagerly traded with Loring and the others just a couple of months before were gone.[1] They had been ordered to replace men in the dwindling ranks of infantry regiments. Replacing those men as prison guards were those not fit for field duty.

Under the worsening conditions the number of fatalities in the prison increased. Being sent to the hospital was more of a death sentence than remaining in the camp. At least inside the camp you might be lucky enough to have a friend to help nurse you or provide what he could in the way of food scraps. With such desperate conditions came desperate plans for escape. Among the six hundred men from Camp Tyler, forty decided to make a run for it, all on the same night.

With little understanding of the area and no provisions, all forty were recaptured with the exception of a few who died during the escape.[2] As punishment for this mass exodus Colonel Gillespie added to the suffering. In the face of a torrential storm Gillespie forced all prisoners out of their sheds. Confederate captain Mason protested this indirect torture but Gillespie ignored his protests. Throughout the night men wandered about in groups seeking what shelter they could find; some men leaned against each other, some sought relief on the lee side of their sheds. Soaked, cold, shivering, and in a horrific state of health, this was the death blow for many. Throughout the night and early morning Loring could only watch as his comrades suffered. September 8 dawned as the storm subsided. Loring recalled that one year ago exactly he had been aboard the USS *Weehawken* firing upon Fort Moultrie in the shadow of Fort Sumter.[3] He thought to himself how much his fortune had changed.

Colonel Gillespie continued to seek ways to punish the men for their audacity and was convinced that Loring was the instigator behind the escapes. In an attempt to discredit Loring and turn his fellow officers against him, Gillespie decreed that "all well officers must hereafter take nightly lodgings in the main shed."[4] This had a direct impact on the three highest ranking officers in Camp Groce, Lieutenant Colonel Flory, Captain DeHart, and Lieutenant Loring. Flory and DeHart were furious at this latest act of tyranny. They strongly protested and were finally able to strike a deal. They would be able to stay in their quarters as long as they agreed to not attempt to escape. Loring, however, would not agree to this, and as such he was forced to sleep in the overcrowded main shed each night.[5]

Each new day Loring would rise with the sun, wrap his threadbare blanket about him, and step into the yard. He was happy to be alive and able to walk away from that night's torpid torture chamber. The offer was made again. Loring would be paroled and have the option to stay in the officer's quarters as long as he would give his word to not attempt to escape. He refused.

Each night Loring was escorted back to the main shed by two guards. As soon as the guards left, however, Loring silently slipped out the back. He crept through the camp and climbed through the window of the officers' shed, spending the night stretched out on the floorboards. Just before sunrise he carefully found his way back to the enlisted men's shed. Under the watchful eyes of the sentries, Loring would emerge and stretch as he greeted the new day, no one the wiser. Each subsequent day the offer to be allowed to remain in the officers' shed was made, and each day Loring emphatically declined.

The evening ritual of sneaking out of the main shed and into the officers' shed became almost routine. While creeping through camp each night Loring observed the location of the sentries, when the watch would change, and the level of awareness each of the guards exhibited. Over several nights Loring began to recognize patterns. He saw gaps in the field of view the guards had of the yard and noted that certain guards were prone to lapses of attention.

During conversations with the guards, Loring was able to ascertain that a majority of Texans were being recruited as cavalry and sent to Arkansas for service.[6] Based on this information, Loring conceived a plan to impersonate a Confederate cavalryman from a Texas regiment being sent home on furlough to refit his mount. After only a week back in Camp Groce, Loring had a plan to escape.

Armed with a forged pass and a story about returning home to remount for his cavalry unit, Loring waited alone until dark.[7] After dark he slipped through a hole in the back of the enlisted men's shed. He retrieved a huge corn dodger and an improvised Confederate uniform hidden under the corner of the shed. Slowly, quietly he slunk through the camp toward the wall. All he needed to do was slip through the wall near where he and de Doe had done so previously.

Peering from behind a water barrel, Loring could see the wall. As he started to move from behind the barrel some movement caught his attention out of the corner of his eye. Spying up at the top of the wall, Loring could see a dimly lit figure in the sentry box. The guard seemed to be more attentive than usual and was staring directly toward his location. Loring waited. The sentry turned to face the opposite direction. Loring took two steps from behind the barrel and again looked up at the sentry box. The outline of a second man in the box was barely visible. Loring was stunned. As the second sentry began to turn, Loring leaped back behind the barrel.

Making it to the wall was supposed to be the easiest part of the escape, and Loring had already been foiled twice. He was beginning to have doubts as he watched and waited. With both guards facing away from him and engaged in conversation, Loring saw his chance and took it. Keeping as low as possible he sprinted to the corner of the wall. He slid to a stop in the tall grass just inside the dead line. Peering back through the grass, a shiver went down his spine.

Captain DeHart had just rounded the corner, headed to the sinks. The captain bumping into Loring could have caused enough of a commotion to alert the sentries. Loring's heart was pounding and sweat ran down his forehead. He tried to control his breathing and calm himself. Wasting no time, Loring slithered through the tall grass toward the wall and the loose board. After what seemed an eternity, he reached the board. Pulling on the board, it budged only slightly. He tried again. The board moved toward him but only a foot. Not enough to crawl through. It did, however, provide just enough of an incline that he could climb the board and jump the fence.

As Loring stood to climb the board a voice rang out: " Cop'rl er the guard! Cop'rl er the guard!"[8] A sentry less than one hundred feet away was alerted that something was wrong. Loring dropped back down and hugged the ground. He was so close to escaping.

In an instant he made the decision to fight another day. In one motion he kicked the board back into place as he turned. His feet dug into the dry Texas dirt, seeking the traction needed to put as much distance as possible between him, the wall, and the sentries. If caught he would be inside the dead line and the sentries were sure to open fire. With his life on the line, Loring kept as low as possible and sprinted back to the corner of his shed. The sentries were at full alert. Loring could hear the pounding of boots on the ground. Sergeants were yelling orders as the clang of bayonets being fixed to muskets echoed in the night. Guards rushed into the prison.

Loring ripped off his makeshift confederate uniform, wrapped the corn dodger in it, and threw this under the corner of the shed. He dove through the back window, stretched out on the floor, and tried to calm his breathing. Thirty seconds later a squad of guards came through the prison gate to search the sheds. A corporal followed by two guards crashed through the shed door and held up his lantern. Loring propped himself up on one elbow. He stared blankly at the intruders as if he had just been rudely woken from dreams of home and freedom. Other prisoners protested, swearing at the guards.

The next day rumors abounded regarding the previous night's commotion. Two days later Loring learned that the guard had been doubled to train new recruits. He would wait for another opportunity.

21

Deadliest Killer

Yellow fever is highly contagious and known to afflict those living in close quarters. It is a horrific disease with symptoms that include headaches, chills, nausea, and fever.[1] (Unknown to the populace of Loring's time, the disease is spread by infected mosquitos. Until an effective vaccine was developed in the 1930s, yellow fever could be fatal.) In the final stages of the disease victims would experience severe abdominal cramping, their skin would turn yellow and they would vomit black blood. Half of those exhibiting these symptoms would die. It was deadlier than any battle or guard with a fixed bayonet.

When an outbreak of the deadly disease occurred in Galveston, Colonel Gillespie knew that the best way to avoid it was to move away from those infected. The best course of action to prevent the disease from spreading among his soldiers and prisoners was to put some distance between the camp and the nearest outbreak. With only a few minutes' notice, Gillespie gave the order to move the camp. The prisoners filed out of their sheds and were forced to march toward an undisclosed location.

Officers were allowed to walk at their own pace. The two hundred men too sick or unable to walk were loaded into wagons along with what little baggage the prisoners called their own. With Colonel Gillespie leading the way, 750 prisoners marched toward the horizon.[2] Five hours later the bedraggled line of prisoners found themselves on the banks of the Brazos River, where they were ferried across. Once across the prisoners were allowed to rest for the night and cook whatever food they had.

The next morning the march began anew. Under a scorching sun the men plodded across open ground for ten miles. The line of stragglers extended for over a half mile. Malnourished and dehydrated men fell along the roadside. At the end of the day the order was again given to halt. For an additional two hours men dragged themselves into the makeshift camp. Those stragglers who staggered into camp often just sagged to the ground and did not move until the next morning. There were no walls, no dead lines, and no sheds. The wide-open space spread to the horizon. This was the new prison.

22

Making the Best of It

With no water other than what the men had been able to carry, Colonel Gillespie sent out a party of guards to search the area for a water source. They were not gone long. A stream ran only three hundred yards away. The prison camp moved closer to the water.

The Union prisoners were told to make camp in the sandy, swampy creek bottom. Prisoners complained as they swatted at the clouds of mosquitos in the low-lying area. The Union officers were paroled and allowed to make their camp on the banks of the creek bed. Loring, being the only relatively well and fit person in his mess, erected a crude shelter for his suffering comrades. It was minimal but provided some relief from the heat of the day and the cool damp of the night.

The stream itself was no more than a trickle of muddy water with a few places where the water pooled. With no other choice, the men filled their canteens. The Confederate guards and officers, having little concern for the prisoners downstream, "stirred the brook and made our drinking place muddy; contaminated the upper puddles with the rinsings of their filthy persons and their wash clothes, whence it oozed down to us an abominable, poisonous concoction."[1]

Despite some loud protests from Loring and other prisoners Gillespie forbade the prisoners from going upstream of the Confederates to fetch their drinking water. Disgusted, Loring devised a system to at least provide some cleaner water for consumption. Using a tin cup he dug a hole in the bottom of the stream and buried a small barrel in it with the lip of the barrel just below the surface of the water. This helped to collect cleaner water in the barrel. The heavier particulates were carried down farther in the water column and were blocked from entering. It was an improvement. Even those rebels who were muddying the water upstream recognized that this was an improvement and liberally partook of this fountain of cleaner water.

Word spread throughout the surrounding countryside that the 750 men from Camp Groce prison had been relocated nearby to avoid the yellow fever epidemic. Curious local citizens took the opportunity to come out and see for themselves a real Billy Yank and the entire spectacle. What they saw shocked and horrified them. The condition of the men was terrible. Hardly recognizable, the men were mere skeletons of their former selves, with rags hanging from their starving limbs. In response many good people in the name of their Christian ideals began to send charitable gifts of food and clothing to the prisoners. Even though these were loyal southerners from Texas, they were also compassionate people. They sent "milk, eggs, bread, potatoes, a little butter." One German sent a horse to bring Lieutenant Colonel Flory to his home so that "once more [he] could enjoy the luxury of two good square meals."[2]

This generosity seemed to rival the contagion of the yellow fever. Confederate captain Mosely told Loring that he was headed to Hempstead. He would make it a point to see the provost marshal there and would attempt to retrieve Loring's gold watch and some of the money that was taken from him when he was first captured. Captain Mosely kept his word, and several days later he presented Loring with his watch, his watch chain, and thirty dollars.[3] Thanking Mosely, Loring offered the captain his last piece of Union naval clothing, a uniform vest. Mosely declined. Loring again offered the vest but this time suggested that in return he be allowed to have a large pan to be filled with sugar. Mosely, who was a kindhearted fellow, accepted and agreed to look the other way.

Sugar was a rare and precious commodity. Loring secured it from a compassionate patron who had frequented the camp, in trade for his watch. He mixed the sugar with the regular ration of cornmeal to make a mush. Loring had this distributed to those who were in the greatest need throughout the camp. But as the weeks passed the number of visitors declined and the amount of charitable donations dwindled.

With rations cut and little to nothing to supplement them from the citizenry, Loring's own health began to decline. His hopes and dreams of escape in order to once again report for duty had buoyed his spirits. But he had to make a decision. Either escape while he still had enough strength to reasonably make the attempt or stay and help his comrades in arms in their most desperate hour. Loring mulled the decision. He desperately wanted to get back in the fight and defeat the enemy who kept men such as Jolly Jeff in shackles. Yet he also knew it was his duty to look after his men. As the commanding officer of a ship, essentially its captain, he was considered the senior officer in the camp. He felt it was his duty to look after all the men within the prisons confines, but he had to stay healthy enough to do so. He longed to escape and report for duty but knew he must look after his men first. "Hope deferred maketh the heart sick."[4]

On October 2 the prisoners were told to prepare to move to a healthier place.[5] Loring packed up his few possessions as the men fell in line to begin the long march to the latest undisclosed healthy location. As an officer Loring was paroled for the march and was allowed to walk with various companions.

As the line of march passed houses and farms Loring took the opportunity to stop and visit some of the local people who had been so generous in providing food and clothing to the men. Taking advantage of passing one such house, he stopped and, after knocking on the door, was introduced to Mr. Koch. Loring enjoyed the visit and after some lengthy discussion and subtle persuasion Mr. Koch gave Loring a gallon of milk, some butter, and biscuits for the men. Mr. Koch wished Loring well as he bade him goodbye. As Loring left the house and turned into the road, there was not another person in sight. He had completely lost track of time. The entire line of march had passed him by and left him with an incredible opportunity to escape. However, he had made a decision to see his men through this most difficult time, and without thinking twice about escape he cut cross-country to catch up with the men.

Loring moved out. He cut through several woodlots and then intersected the road. He saw no one. The road didn't even look as though a large group of men had recently passed by. Thinking that he had somehow gotten ahead of the column, he waited. After an hour there was still no sign of the prison column. Loring climbed a tree for a better view. In the distance in the opposite direction from what Loring had expected, a faint cloud could be seen rising up. It was the dust kicked up by over 750 men shuffling along in a column.

Loring backtracked, limping eleven miles, and finally caught up to his comrades. The gallon milk jug was empty and the firkin of butter had melted. He gave the remaining biscuits to a few men as he fell in line with the column. Footsore and tired, Loring and the column passed a small house with two women at the gate who were verbally harassing the Union prisoners as they passed by. One woman yelled toward Loring, "Don't you think you'd er better stayd tr hum?" Loring replied, "Perhaps! There's no place like home; and the more of Texas I see the more home is good enough for me—particularly if one is to die of starvation." To this the woman exclaimed, "Well! Why didn't you stay there then?" Tired and in no mood for harassing conversation, Loring saucily rebuked her. "Why? From curiosity to view a Texan Lady at short range, but we are wearying of the long unsuccessful search. Good bye!"[6]

By dark the column had covered fifteen miles. Loring had walked nearly twice that. The column was halted for the night among a grove of oak trees owned by a Northern sympathizer. There was a small stream of clear, cool water and a few haystacks for bedding. This was all a prisoner could hope for. The men slumped to the ground, many falling asleep where they fell. Morning came early and the march resumed for another five miles to Chappell Hill.[7]

As the soldiers marched through town they passed a bakery. The baker was standing in the doorway watching the scraggly crew shuffle past. Loring shouted out and offered ten Confederate dollars for any bread or cookies. The baker simply barked back, "NO!" They continued on through town and at noon the column halted. They had arrived at the new healthy place: a swamp!

23

The Swamp

Loring was sure Colonel Gillespie chose this location specifically to inflict misery and suffering upon the men. Why else would he have the prison moved to a swamp? To Loring's point, there was a grove of pecan trees with two springs of clean water and sheds used during the harvest on higher ground. But this area was to be used exclusively by the Confederates, while the prisoners were forced onto the banks of "a miasmatic swamp."[1]

The prisoners struggled for their very survival. Even the Confederate surgeon attached to the prison made his opinion clear on the topic. "Medical skill cannot work miracles; . . . that neither he nor any other man can successfully cope with the miasmatic emanations from such a hole."[2] Assistant Surgeon H. L. Rugely of the First Texas Heavies made it clear that under such wretched conditions he would not be held responsible for the health and welfare of the prisoners.

Loring and the other officers were given a choice as to where they would build their shelter. They chose to build on higher ground. For the next couple of days Loring and the rest of the prison population worked to erect crude shelters from whatever resources they could find.

Most of the men were sick. All of them were undernourished. Those who had been too sick to walk to this new place arrived by wagon. Five died in the backs of the wagons. With no food or water to be had, many others hovered near death.

Loring was still the only well person in his mess. With his shelter completed, he turned his full attention to trying to secure some food from the surrounding countryside. He took advantage of being paroled and scoured the area for a sympathetic soul. On his first foray he came across a slave and begged for a piece of bread, but the man had none. The next day the same slave appeared at camp with freshly baked biscuits from a lady who lived not more than two miles away. Loring thought that "here was a friend worth cultivating."[3] He sent word to the woman asking for an opportunity to introduce himself; a day later a response arrived. Miss E. Posey Traynham accepted and granted permission for Loring to visit.

Not wanting to waste an opportunity to meet a possible source of sustainable food, Loring set out the next day to meet Miss Traynham. With his parole secured to leave camp as long as he returned by dark, Loring walked the two miles to the home of Miss Posey and her father, Dr. Traynham. Arriving at midmorning, Loring was disappointed to find that Miss Posey was not at home. However, the young lady had left word with her father that she might have a caller, so Dr. Traynham was not surprised by this Northern visitor.

Not sure what to expect, Loring was cordially invited to dine with the doctor. The two men were from very different places and of very different political views. Dr. Traynham was originally from South Carolina, the very birthplace of secession. He was a widower and was quite sympathetic to the Southern cause. However, the two men managed to carry on a very lively discussion over the next two hours. At the conclusion of dinner, the doctor was kind enough to provide Loring with a bottle of milk, some butter, a lump of opium for the sick, and a pair of trousers. Loring thanked the doctor for his hospitality and generosity. As he turned to leave, Dr. Traynham invited him to stop by to visit each day.

Loring headed back to camp. Arriving at his shelter, he found no one on the banks of the swamp. The entire prison population had been forced down into the swamp by Colonel Gillespie to prevent any escape attempts.[4] This was ridiculous. There had been no escape attempts; the men were too weak to try. Loring protested to anyone who would hear him, but his protests fell on deaf ears.

Loring looked down into the swamp. Dirty, squalid faces with empty eyes stared back at him. The men were despondent. They sat on little tufts of dry ground created by upturned tree roots. These tiny islands would accommodate two or three men at the most. As far as Loring could see there were islands of men staring up at him from a sea of misery. Loring was forced to join the rest of the men in the swamp as night approached. There was nothing they could do for lodging. Loring parsed out the small amount of rations provided by Dr. Traynham to those who needed it the most. The men were grateful and it lifted their spirits. But as the sun sank into the swamp the mosquitos emerged. Clouds of the blood-sucking tormentors descended on the suffering men.

Throughout the night Loring slogged through the muck, moving among the men to check on them. One poor fellow, Paymaster's Clerk Fanning, was so sick he was hallucinating. Fanning would yell out, "Lt. Loring is trying to kill me! Stop him! He is trying to poison me!"[5] Loring unsuccessfully tried to reassure Fanning that he was in no way trying to harm him.

An eerie fog rolled in and blanketed the swamp with a dense, wet veil. The coughing and groans of the suffering prisoners echoed in the mist. The voices of Confederate guards singing about killing Yankees rolled down the banks into the swamp and added to the cacophony of misery. Twice during the long night Loring stumbled and fell over the bodies of men who had died as he tried to provide relief and comfort.[6] The fog slowly burned off the following morning to reveal small parties of men digging fresh graves for their comrades.

On October 6 Loring received word that the *Wave*'s master at arms, "a man of noteworthy gladiatorial physique; in the prime of manly strength and vigor," had perished during the night.[7] Loring had talked with this man just a few days earlier. Why were so many men being lost? It just made no sense. They were being punished by Gillespie, a tyrant who sought revenge for his mistreatment in a Northern prison camp. Loring became despondent over the conditions and the loss of so many fine men he had served with and had come to know and admire.

In the weeks since the men had been forced into the swamp Loring had seen three men from his own mess die. If the men were allowed to move up slope just one hundred feet, out of the swamp onto dry ground where there was a breeze to keep some of the mosquitos at bay, he was sure some of this could have been avoided. With conditions at their worst, many men felt that to stay in the swamp meant certain death. Even in their feverish, starved state they would rather risk escape and the hostile countryside than to surely die as prisoners.

A few days later, after the sun had set, Ensign Rogers slipped through the guard and into the night. He was recaptured the next day. Two days later Ensign Howard (de Doe), in his feeble state, did the same but failed.[8] He was picked up at gunpoint only a few miles away. The guard was reinforced with twenty men.

Just days later, Confederate general John G. Walker visited the prison camp.[9] Standing at the top of the bank, he peered down in the swamp and surveyed the situation. Loring attempted to climb the bank to approach General Walker but was shoved back down and at bayonet point told to keep his mouth shut. Without so much as even descending the bank or setting one foot in the swamp General Walker declared it quite appropriate. He proclaimed that Colonel Gillespie had everything in order.

Loring was sure that General Walker was not aware that of the two hundred original men imprisoned in Camp Groce, including the men captured from the *Wave* and *Granite City*, all but seventy-one had died while in the care of Colonel Gillespie and the Confederacy.

24

Tied Up

L ife in the swamp was barely tolerable. Each day Loring would leave camp on parole, in search of food for his comrades. Every day he would return with a few items. He distributed the food to those men who needed it the most to supplement their rations of parched corn and rotten bacon.

On October 20 Loring left camp and walked to Dr. Traynham's plantation for the last time.[1] When he arrived he was disappointed to find that Dr. Traynham was not at home. He was, however, pleasantly surprised to find Miss Posey at home entertaining two other young ladies. Miss Posey introduced Loring to the Stone sisters from Chappell Hill.

Loring was not expecting this. He was suddenly embarrassed by his appearance. "His garments hung upon his once plump figure 'like a shirt upon a handspike.' His bashful toes protruded from gaping holes in his shoes and his bare skin blushed through openings in his trousers."[2] The young women feigned not noticing the lieutenant's dirty and tattered appearance. They began to banter back and forth with each other and Loring. As they ate and drank, Loring relished the conversation regarding the war. He even led the ladies in singing "The Star-Spangled Banner." The afternoon flew by.

The frivolity ended as the sun began to sink toward the horizon. Loring's sense of duty required that he return to his suffering comrades in the swamp. With an armload of food and a bottle of milk, Loring thanked Miss Posey and the Stone sisters for their hospitality and generosity.

On the walk back to the primordial prison in the swamp, Loring realized how unfair and ridiculous it was to allow only officers the privilege of parole, which in this case was a decided advantage for survival. As Loring strode into camp he walked up to Confederate captain Mosely and held out his parole pass. Mosely took the pass and, with eyebrows raised, looked at Loring. Loring stared back at the captain and stated clearly in a loud voice, "I am giving up my privilege of parole until all men are paroled from the prison during the day." Mosely smiled and handed the pass back to Loring. Loring would not take it and declared, "Parole all or none!"[3] He walked down the bank into the swamp. The men in the swamp saw what was happening and began to cheer Loring while yelling obscenities at Mosely and the other guards.

Loring's act of defiance put Captain Mosely and the prison on alert. At dusk two guards walked down the bank to the edge of the swamp and told Loring to follow them. Loring was led to a large oak tree away from the swamp where none of the other prisoners could see what was happening. Waiting under the tree was a Confederate lieutenant. Yelling to a sergeant, the lieutenant called out, "Bring them ropes! Come. Stand up here!"[4] The lieutenant offered Loring the parole pass. Loring steadfastly refused, reiterating that all should be paroled or none. His request was denied.

The lieutenant turned Loring around. He grabbed Loring's arms and pulled his hands behind his back, tying them together. One of the guards then doubled the knot. Looking up, Loring estimated the lowest tree branch to be ten feet overhead. Expecting the worst, Loring swallowed hard. He thought, "Is this how it is going to end? They are going to hang me for refusing to be paroled." Loring looked over his shoulder as a guard moved close.

A second guard walked up behind Loring brandishing something. With a quick flick of his wrists he threw a thin blanket over Loring's shoulders. The lieutenant, sergeant, and two guards turned and left Loring standing under the tree. The lieutenant called back to Loring, "Safe bind safe find."[5] Loring sank to the ground and leaned back against the tree, relieved to be under it instead of swinging from it.

Loring looked toward the guards thirty feet away. He could barely make out their forms in the darkness. If he could barely see them that meant they could barely see him. Loring had spent decades aboard various seagoing vessels. During his years at sea he had become very nimble in the art of knot tying. A good seaman could tie and untie a knot in the dark, without looking at the rope and with numb fingers. Under the cover of the blanket Loring untied the knots from behind his back. He placed the small rope in his pocket for the night.

Waking up before the guards, Loring pulled the rope from his pocket. He made a loop on each end of the rope and slipped his hands through these. Reaching down, he slid the rope over his knees and then his feet so his hands were behind his back. He rolled his wrists and the rope appeared tight. A few minutes later one of the guards poked Loring with the tip of his boot. Loring rolled over and sat up. The blanket fell from his shoulders, exposing his hands, still apparently tied behind his back. The guard helped him to his feet and untied the knot.

Once untied Loring immediately found Captain Mosely and loudly protested being tied up like a common criminal. Mosely explained that if Loring would accept the parole pass this treatment would cease. Loring refused. Again at dusk two guards escorted Loring to the tree. They bound his hands behind him and threw the old blanket over him. Loring again slipped out of the knots of his captors and then retied the rope before dawn. This continued for several nights.

One evening in the midst of a terrible thunderstorm, Captain Mosely ventured out to the oak tree where Loring was tied up.[6] Mosely pleaded with Loring to accept the parole so that he could at least crawl under his crude shelter to shield him from the elements. Loring protested, reminding the captain that he would accept his parole only if all the men were paroled.

Mosely told Loring he could not do that. It was beyond his authority. He pleaded with Loring and explained that as a Christian man he could not bear to think of Loring suffering under such conditions. He would personally be grateful if Loring would accept the pass and seek shelter. Loring told him he would do no such thing. He would, however, agree to remain under the tree if Mosely would have him untied. Mosely agreed. As the captain walked away Loring yelled, "I will see you in the morning." Loring kept his word. The next evening at dusk the guards did not come to escort Loring to the oak tree.

Without his parole Loring could not venture out to the countryside. After a week of not making his rounds several of the locals began to inquire with the prison officials about Loring's well-being. As Loring was making repairs to his shelter in the swamp he heard a familiar female voice. Looking up the bank Loring saw Captain Mosely escorting a local woman and her two daughters, the Stone sisters.[7] Captain Mosely pointed down in the swamp and said to the ladies, "There is your precious Lieutenant Loring." They waved. Having made sure with their own eyes that he was still among the living, they moved on. Loring was only as well and good as one could expect under such circumstances. His health was better than that of the others in the camp, and he attributed that to being from hardy New England stock. But he also knew that being able to leave the camp daily on parole had helped him avoid some of the disease rampant among the men.

On October 30 word came from the guards to prepare to march to an unknown destination.[8] The wagons were brought up and loaded with those too infirm to walk. The men were ordered into a line of march. Starved and sick, they could barely move as the column crept along the road. Men too exhausted to continue would fall off to the side of the road. Some would never stand again and were buried where they fell.

The column proceeded past Dr. Traynham's plantation and the doctor himself stood at the gate with a pail of cool, fresh water. Dr. Traynham offered the men a drink as they limped past. Loring strode up to the gate. Dr. Traynham recognized Loring, offered him a drink, and invited him into the house to say goodbye to Miss Posey. The sentry posted at the gate denied Loring entry despite Dr. Traynham's protests. Loring thanked Dr. Traynham for his kindness and gifts of food for his men. He bid the doctor farewell knowing that he would never see him or Miss Posey again. Loring took one final drink of water from the Traynham well and joined his comrades in the dusty line of march.

Dark found the men three miles from the swamp. They filed into a grove of oaks and the men lit fires and cooked what little they had. As the fires glowed, distant thunder could be heard as a storm approached. Within minutes the skies opened and a deluge fell upon them. Men huddled together under the trees but were soaked almost immediately. The storm raged throughout the night as prisoners straggled into camp. A wagonload of the sick pulled into camp in the early morning with one of its occupants dead.[9] The rest were too weak to help themselves and lay in an inch of water in the wagon bed.

At the break of dawn Loring went ahead of the column toward Chappell Hill to see if he could secure some "Lincoln Coffee."[10] He inquired with a slave about some coffee and the man obliged, pointing at a house. Loring knocked on the door and was met by the wife of a local minister. He asked if she could please spare some coffee for some of his men. Happy to help the sick and suffering, she boiled coffee and prepared some breakfast. Loring offered her some Confederate scrip but the woman refused. He walked the two miles back to the column with a bountiful breakfast and real coffee in his canteen for his men.

The men nearly swallowed the food whole, washing it down with the coffee. They filed back into the line of march and headed toward Chappell Hill. The line led to the train station, where they boarded open cars for the presumed ride back to Camp Groce.

With the cars loaded the engineer gave the locomotive some steam to coax it ahead. There was a slight incline in the track at the station, and despite the engineer's best efforts the train didn't budge. The engineer called for more wood to build steam. Still the dilapidated, rusted hulk could not pull the load.

An order rang out for all those who could walk to get off the train and push.[11] The train backed up. As it slowly approached the station and the slight incline a hundred prisoners fell to its side and pushed. The train barely made it up the incline and began to pick up speed. The men struggled to jump aboard. During the ride back to Camp Groce the men were forced to get off on two other occasions to push the train over some nearly imperceptible incline in the track. Barely able to maintain four miles per hour, the train seemingly took forever to reach Camp Groce.

Reaching the station just outside of Camp Groce, the train discharged its filthy cargo. Loring and his men stumbled through the gates of the prison. They felt a strange sense of relief that they had survived the nightmare in the swamp. But as the echo of the gates closing behind them reverberated through the camp Loring knew he would need to find a way out. His survival would depend on it.

25

The Power of the Pen (cil)

Nearly one-third of the prisoners who had inhabited the camp were dead from disease, starvation, and abuse. It was November 1, 1864, and Loring was once again confined in Camp Groce. Something about the camp haunted Loring. He had tried so hard to help his men survive this ordeal. There had been opportunities to just walk away from the swamp and escape but his commitment to his men was too strong to leave them in their greatest hour of need. Now Loring's health had declined and he knew that if he was going to survive he would need to escape. He struggled with the decision, which meant he would have to leave his men.

Loring woke the next morning with a renewed vigor that was palpable. As he walked through the camp checking on his men a Union infantry officer, Lt. Col. Aaron Flory of the Forty-Sixth Indiana, approached him. He quipped, "I think, Captain you mean to leave us before long!" Loring smiled and responded, "And you?" Flory enthusiastically replied, "Will you take me with you?"[1] Loring stopped where he stood and a very serious conversation ensued between the two men.

Loring clearly and directly explained to the colonel the danger and severity of the hardship that would be involved in such a journey. Loring also knew that in ten days there would be a full moon. This would be an ideal time to escape and nothing would stand in his way of making it to Union lines to report for duty. Flory understood completely, and the two officers began to strategize.

For several days Loring and Flory planned and plotted their escape route. Loring suggested that the pair escape by way of Shreveport, Louisiana. Flory countered, recommending they head toward Brashear City near Berwick's Bay in Louisiana.[2] He knew the area well, having seen action there with his regiment. The men agreed they would head to Berwick's Bay, 350 miles away as the crow flies.

As the prisoners settled into a routine the guards became complacent. Loring and Flory continued to plan. Their first challenge would be to cross the vast, trackless Texas wilderness. No paths or roads to follow. Flory expressed his concern about how they would navigate at night without a map or compass. Loring reassured Flory. As long as he could see the night sky he would use the heavens to guide them.

Loring's greatest concern was how they would actually exit the prison and what provisions they could scrape together to eat for the first few days. Loring also had a personal concern, his footwear. His boots were so badly worn that his toes stuck out the ends and the soles flopped when he walked. This was resolved the next day when one of Loring's men died and he inherited his boots.

The boots were made of good-quality calf leather, but they were three sizes too big. Loring wore two pairs of woolen socks he had kept hidden away. He stuffed anything he could find into the toes for a better fit. With a three-hundred- to four-hundred-mile march on the horizon, ill-fitting boots was an issue to consider. Having no better alternative, Loring made do.

Just a couple of days prior to the escape Loring learned that one of their favorite companions, Paymaster Fanning from the *Wave*, had died. John Reed, the paymaster from the *Granite City*, gained permission to travel to the hospital in Hempstead to collect Fanning's personal belongings and attempt to make sure that Fanning's grave was marked. At the hospital all Reed found was a bundle of rags. Attached to a button was a torn piece of paper with a barely legible note, "Fannin Yankee." Reed approached the nearest rebel and protested such treatment of the dead. He asked where Fanning was buried. The rebel remarked, that he didn't know. "I got no time to waste on explanations, waiting for a fellow who is just about to kick the bucket."[3] The comment sent a shiver down Reed's spine. Could it be that the rebels were "ditching" men before they had expired? Reed returned to Camp Groce with the sad and infuriating news.

Loring's luck began to change. Two days prior to the escape ninety-two dollars in greenbacks were returned to him by the provost marshal, Captain McDade. The money had been confiscated six months before during roll call on the first day in Camp Groce. Loring was ecstatic with the windfall. He offered the money to his messmates to help sustain them in the coming days.

Loring and Flory bartered for provisions as they prepared their kit for the upcoming sojourn. Flory noted that one of the rebel guards had an eye for shiny Federal coat buttons and so he cut the buttons from his uniform coat and bartered for a gold half eagle. In turn he traded this for Mexican silver dollars.

November was cold and winter was fast approaching. Temperatures routinely dropped below freezing at night. During the day the men sought any material that might provide some insulation or that could be used to make a bed to keep them off the cold dirt floor. At night the men simply had to endure as they shivered beneath their threadbare blankets.

Loring noticed that several ingenious prisoners were taking advantage of the thick grass in an overgrown cornfield just outside the prison walls. These men requested passes to go out and cut the tall grass, as it made excellent insulation for bedding.[4] They used their blankets to haul the grass back to their sheds.

The turn in the weather combined with the lack of proper nutrition caused a rise in the number of men taken to the hospital. In just three days, fifty-six men were hospitalized.[5] During the morning roll call only 408 men were present out of the original 800. Loring knew that if he were to stay the odds of survival were stacked against him. He and Flory made final preparations for escape.

Loring's experience from his previous escape attempt was invaluable. To support themselves the first few days they scrounged together "15 pounds of biscuits, 1-pound each of coffee and sugar, 3-pounds of bacon, a little salt, a lot of matches."[6] They would need to get as far away as they could as quickly as possible. It would be important to keep moving and not have to stop to forage for food.

Loring and Flory would be dressed as Confederate soldiers. Their kit included "a pair of blankets each, . . . a large enameled cloth, . . . a Mexican serape, an old iron 2-tined fork . . . a rusty table knife, a tin cup, a tin plate, two enameled cloth knapsacks, a pillow-case bag, and the colonel's canteen."[7]

Loring had memorized the route they would follow: they would travel twenty-five miles north toward Huntsville, staying out of sight and traveling only at night, then head east one hundred miles across the Texas prairie toward Livingston. They would cross two forks of the San Jacinto River and the Grand Cane, Trinity and Neches Rivers. Then they would turn south and follow the Sabine River to Ballou's Ferry before heading due east five miles above Orange, Texas, and five miles below Nibletts Bluff, Louisiana. From there they would head to Lake Charles City on the Calcasieu River, then to Mermentau, Vermillion, New Iberia, Jeanerette, Franklin, Centerville, Pattersonville, and Berwicks Bay, entering Union lines at Brashear City.

The distance to be traveled was only one of the challenges. The men were sure to encounter all types of people who would inquire as to who they were, where they were headed, and why. They would need passes and papers proving who they were. Loring enlisted the help of one of the other officers in camp to forge passes. Upon inspection of the completed passes, Loring found them to be impeccable. His read, "Headquarters Anderson's Battalion. Rusk, Texas, Nov. 12th 1864 Special Order No. 30. Private B.S Henderson is hereby detached to proceed to his home near Vermillion Parish, La. To remount himself, to return within thirty days or be considered a deserter. By order Scott Anderson, Col: Com'dg. L.G. Etheridge. Lt." On the opposite side of the order was written, "Nacogdoches, Texas. Examined and permitted to pass as per within order. E.F. Brown Capt. & Provost Marshal."[8]

To complete the ruse both men took false names. Loring would assume the name Henderson and Flory would assume the name Miller. To ensure that the papers would pass close inspection Loring had the signatures on the passes signed by different men with different shades of ink. The passes would be extremely important but only if the men actually escaped from the prison.

To accomplish this Loring and Flory devised an ingenious and clever plan. They decided to not risk escape by crawling through or climbing over the wall between armed sentries. Instead, with steely nerve, they would walk right out the front gate, right past the guards, in broad daylight.

The Power of the Pen(cil)

They would do this by capitalizing on the thick, lush grass growing right outside the prison walls. They would go out to gather grass for bedding but would simply not return. In order to do so they needed passes to allow them outside. Loring made two copies of a smuggled pass with the nub of his lead pencil. The pass would be presented to the guards at the main gate of the prison and with any luck Loring and Flory would begin their walk home. The pass read, "Head Qtrs, Camp Groce Nov 13/64 Captain Loring has permission to pass out for the day. H.E. Mosely, Fed Prisoners."[9] Flory's pass was the same but in his name. Loring thought, if this works then the pencil is definitely mightier than the sword.

On November 13, 1864, at 3:00 p.m. Ensign Latham, the executive officer from the *Wave*, and Engineer Green from the *Granite City* walked up to the main gate and presented the guards with their passes to go out and gather grass. They carried a couple of loosely rolled-up blankets and a pillowcase. These appeared empty but were filled with a portion of the food provisions for Loring and Flory. One hour later Loring walked toward the main gate with a loosely rolled blanket. On his way toward the gate he passed Flory, seated on a chunk of wood near his shed. As Loring passed by Flory called out, loud enough for the guards to hear, "Where are you headed?" Without breaking stride Loring responded, "Oh! I am just going for a little more grass for bedding." Flory retorted, "Hold on, I will go with you! I want some grass too!" Loring answered, "All right; come on, I'll go slowly!"[10]

At the main gate Loring handed the guard his forged pass. The sentry looked at it and handed it to the sergeant. The sergeant examined the pass, checking the date and signatures. He looked Loring in the eye. With no hesitation he handed it back to him. Flory produced his pass. The sergeant took a quick look and waved them both through the gate. With as little emotion as possible the two men walked into the field and stayed close to the edge, which adjoined a nearby forest. Locating Latham and Green, they exchanged some final goodbyes and collected the other half of their provisions. Hidden in the grass, the men silently prayed for darkness to descend.

26

Navigating by the Wind

Loring and Flory were alone in the field as the sun dipped below the horizon and familiar voices from the prison could be heard wafting on the breeze. As the moon began to rise, so too did the two men. They sprinted for the tree line and the forest. At first they were hesitant and darted from tree to tree. Stopping, looking ahead, they listened for any possible Confederate soldier wandering in the woods. They moved to the next bush and the next. As they gained confidence they began to move swiftly. The first few miles flew by as the excitement and the adrenaline rush caused the two men to skip and run as if they were schoolboys.[1] As the night continued the miles drifted by. Flory was light on his feet and Loring needed to focus to keep up with him.

With the sun fully up Loring (aka Henderson) and Flory (aka Miller) had traveled thirty miles. With the adrenaline no longer coursing through their veins they needed to rest. Making a small fire, they boiled water for coffee and ate a biscuit.

The men were anxious to move on but it was dangerous to move during the day. The original plan was to move only at night, but the men wanted to put more miles between them and the prison. Loring and Flory were extra vigilant, as the occasional shot could be heard from locals hunting deer and turkeys in the distance. By sundown they had traveled another sixteen miles. They had covered forty-six miles in twenty-four hours. No small feat. "In a small clump of bushes, convenient to wood and water, a fire was built, a pot of coffee brewed, and a small rasher of bacon boiled, small for it behooved us to early inaugurate an economical system in dispensing the limited rations."[2] Both men gathered some pine boughs and spread them on the ground for bedding. With only a thin blanket each for a covering, they shivered and huddled closer to the dying fire as the temperature dropped. Even so they delighted in knowing that they were shivers of freedom.

November 15 broke with a red sun rising. Loring quipped, "Red sun in morn, sailor take warn." The sun was soon obscured by clouds. This posed a problem. Without a compass they would need to rely heavily upon Loring's vast knowledge of the heavens and his ability to navigate at night. As they began to move they prayed for the sun to show its face, for "under favorable circumstances, sailing by the sun alone is fraught with difficulties which experience alone can overcome, and you need not brand yourself the champion idiot should you circle with its diurnal motion."[3]

Loring had an uncanny ability to estimate the time, usually within just a couple of minutes. At around ten that morning he put that ability to good use. As the sun peeked from behind the clouds for the briefest of moments Loring fixed its position and lined up a distant object on the horizon with the sun's position in the sky. Then, "given the estimated time, multiply the number of hours from noon—the sun then bearing true south—by 15 [degrees], its apparent hourly rate of motion. So many times as the product is contained in 11 [degrees] 15′—the number of degrees and minutes between each compass point, will be the sun's number of points East or West, as the hour may be a.m. or p.m., from the true South."[4]

Loring determined their direction. He then observed the direction of the wind and noticed that it was generally coming out of the southwest. He decided that in order to continue on without the aid of the sun they would navigate by the wind. To continue traveling east, the wind needed to be on their right. "Hence, in sailing East, it must be maintained on our starboard quarter."[5]

Loring continually checked the wind and the direction it pushed the tree branches and then made adjustments to their course as they went. At noon they noticed a change in the terrain. The solid ground gave way to swamps and bayous interlaced with cane fields. Loring told Flory they must be getting close to the San Jacinto River. Progress slowed to a crawl. As they made camp for lunch a rainstorm overtook them. To avoid becoming completely soaked they used a couple of forked sticks with a ridgepole running between them to hang their enameled cloth and provide some shelter from the rain. This kept the men from being directly in the rain, but they shivered on the damp ground as the cold seeped into their bones. Throughout the night they would occasionally leave the shelter and try to warm themselves by the small fire that sputtered in the drizzle.

The morning of November 16 dawned cloudy as the men gathered their kit to begin a new day's march. The rain continued falling, and Loring and Flory were soaked through. Unable to fix their position without the sun, Loring again navigated based on the prevailing wind and headed east.[6] Picking their way through the dense, wet undergrowth, they heard voices nearby. Coming to a very small clearing, they could see a tiny house on the banks of a very long lake. They pushed into thicker cover to avoid being seen. Flory, jumping aside into a bush, hissed at Loring and urgently pointed ahead. Two men with guns were only one hundred feet away and heading right toward them. Loring dove into a bush and watched the approaching strangers as they walked past without seeing the Confederate imposters. Flory suggested they give the house and its occupants a wide berth and take the long way around the lake. Loring nodded in agreement.

The wet, low-lying terrain combined with brambles and thick undergrowth severely impeded their progress. They had gone only eight miles but were nearly played out. Sitting down to eat, they took stock of their food rations. Walking fifty-five miles in three days had caused the men to consume more of their provisions than they had originally planned. Loring was also concerned about his oversized boots. They were already showing signs of serious wear. The toes of the boots looked as though they had been cut with a knife and peeled back.

On November 17, the fourth day, Loring and Flory departed quickly in a rainy, cloudy mist, ready to fight through the brambles and undergrowth. By the end of the day they were shredded, tired, and sore, having ripped their way through just three miles of the worst undergrowth imaginable. Flory gathered wood for a fire and Loring attended to his boots. The welcome smell of boiling coffee and the crackling of the fire lifted their spirits. As the men talked Loring closely inspected his boots. They were torn and ripped with holes where his socks poked through. He had to maintain these and would have to make do with the materials at hand. It would be impossible to continue without some sort of covering for his feet. As he pulled out his pocketknife he recalled his sister Lillie and thought of de Doe and the moccasins he had fashioned for him. Using the knife he cut patches from the enameled cloth and then, with a small sewing kit, he patched the oversized boots.[7] Exhausted, both men fell asleep dreaming of home and loved ones.

November 18 brought more rain and another day filled with battling brambles. Loring had become accustomed to navigating by the wind, but on this morning the wind was variable and the sun still not visible. Rather than chance wandering in circles or becoming completely lost Loring suggested they wait until midday to see if the weather would break and then try and better determine their direction of travel. At noon the weather was still not cooperating. They could no longer wait. The men struck out. Loring, in the lead, told Flory he would follow his instincts. Late that afternoon they stumbled upon a cart path. This provided some much-needed relief from slogging through the heavy undergrowth, but the relief was short-lived. The path became less and less defined until it disappeared "into a hole in the bowels of the earth."[8]

Surrounded by thick vegetation, undergrowth, and dense forest, Loring suggested they camp for the night. As the men made camp a tremendous storm kicked up. Lightning flashed all around them. The men were caught right in the middle of the storm. Hunkering down, they wrapped the enameled cloth around them and squatted down on a hummock. They put their backs up to a large tree and waited. The storm raged on. A searing flash and tremendous clap of thunder louder than the Dahlgren gun on the *Wave* rent the air simultaneously! The men could feel the crash of thunder as it reverberated down the tree through the roots they sat upon. The air was filled with the smell of ozone as the lightning struck not more than one hundred feet away. The men moved away from the tree and burrowed further into the low-lying brush, praying for the storm to subside. Sleep was out of the question.

27

Parched Corn

It was midday but no lighter than twilight due to the clouds. Loring and Flory had not seen the sun in days. Loring had been leading the way by dead reckoning and the direction of the prevailing wind. It made no sense to continue without checking their location and direction of travel. With faces turned upward they looked for a break in the clouds and spent the entire day waiting for better weather. No such luck. Both men were seriously concerned. They had not been able to make much progress through the thick undergrowth and now their provisions were running desperately low. Decisions had to be made. Over the last cup of coffee, Loring and Flory took stock of the few remaining biscuits. They parsed these out to meet two days' short rations. They would need to find some additional sustenance soon. With the decision made to stay another night in this location, Loring made a fire as distant thunder foretold of coming storms.

The next morning the men knocked about camp. At about 10:00 a.m. the clouds parted just enough so that Loring could see the faint outline of the sun. It was enough to fix their position and determine the direction of the wind. They broke camp and began to move.

It had rained the past seven days. The low-lying countryside was flooded. There were a few areas of higher ground as the brambles and undergrowth gave way to a forest of oaks, hickory trees, and squirrels. There were squirrels everywhere! Flory remarked to Loring how a good tree rat makes a fine dinner for a weary traveler. Loring hungrily agreed. But with no gun or trap the men were left to watch the little rodents scamper about. Taking their cue, the hungry men joined the squirrels in search of nuts but found only a few that were bitter and rotten.[1]

The forest again transitioned into a low-lying area where there was standing water from the flooding. This led to cane fields that were partially submerged. Loring and Flory had no choice but to continue. For three miles they waded through the cane fields in water that reached up to their knees. As Loring pushed ahead the earth suddenly fell away and he found himself chest deep in water. Turning around he looked at Flory and deadpanned, "We have arrived at the Trinity River."

The flooded river was too fast to swim. Casting about downstream the pair found a spot where they might be able to cross. A sandbar had formed across one-third of the river. From this point a large tree had fallen partially across and there was a gap of fifteen feet where another tree had fallen down the opposite bank and its leafy branches reached out across the water. They decided to try and cross here. Loring found a long pole and, pushing it into the river bottom, steadied himself on the partially submerged tree. He yelled for Flory to grab him around the waist. Together they crept along the slippery tree with the river current trying to pull them in. Flory held on despite shivering almost uncontrollably. Waist-deep in the raging water, Loring used every ounce of strength to keep them from being swept downstream. Just five feet separated them from the branches of the tree on the opposite bank. Flory yelled to Loring over the rushing water that he was not going to make it. Loring yelled back, "What difference does it make? Rain or river water, we are already wet." With a lunge Loring grabbed at the branches with Flory hanging on tight and the men reached the opposite shore.[2]

Flory was shaking and feverish. They took a moment to collect themselves and take stock of their provisions. They had no food left. They had to find food, and that meant they would need to follow a road, which would inevitably lead to a plantation and an encounter with the local citizenry.

Locating a nearby road they followed it to a field filled with ripe corn. The field was flooded and the stalks stood out like pickets across the landscape. The men could not believe their luck. Plunging ahead, they unrolled their blankets and filled them to capacity with corn. In the distance was a small structure situated on a knoll up out of the water. They headed toward it and as they came closer discovered it was a corncrib. They hoped to sleep inside but found the crib to be stuffed and overflowing with corn. They dumped the corn from their blankets and helped themselves to the dry corn from the crib. With their blankets full, they slung them over their backs and started walking. A half mile beyond the corncrib they settled on a small hummock of dry land and made camp. The roots of an upturned tree provided a small windbreak. Loring used the enameled cloth to rig a shelter, providing a little protection from the inevitable rain.

Flory searched nearby for some dry wood but could find none. The weary travelers marched the half mile back to the corncrib and relieved it of a portion of its roof shakes for kindling. They made the round trip again to help themselves to several of the top rails of a split-rail fence surrounding the cornfield. Secluded under a makeshift shelter and with a fire, the men ate corn. Flory was soon sound asleep.

Loring was tired but could not sleep yet. He needed to tend to his badly worn boots. The toes of the boots were torn open, the heels were twisted sideways, and the boots were three sizes too big. Loring suffered severe blisters. His ankles were sore and at least one toenail had been ripped completely off from blistering. In order to continue he had to make enough repairs each night to make it through the subsequent day, and the only patching material was the enameled cloth. Each night the cloth they used for shelter grew smaller as the patches on Loring's boots grew larger. With the repairs to his boots completed for the night, Loring turned his attention to the corn he and Flory had gathered.

Flory had shucked the ears of corn and then shelled them so that only the kernels were left in the blanket. While Flory slept Loring placed a handful of kernels in the tin cup, then held it over the fire and shook it to keep the kernels from burning. Slowly Loring parched the corn, a handful at a time.[3]

Throughout the night the temperature dropped. The rain turned to hail and then to sleet. The floodwaters developed a skim of ice in the early morning before dawn. Loring woke Flory to get an early start. He did not want to be anywhere nearby when the plantation owner found his corn crib in disarray and part of his split-rail fence missing. Their muddy footprints would be too easy to follow right to the camp. By 4:00 a.m. Loring and Flory were on their way.

The men had to break skim ice as they waded through the flooded landscape. Finding the road, they stayed out of sight and traveled parallel to it until noon. Wet, hungry, and tired, they laid up until dark. After dark they struck out down the road and made good time despite Loring's badly blistered feet. At 2:00 a.m. they burrowed into the thickest brush they could find that was not underwater and made camp. Loring patched his boots while Flory tended to the fire as they each ate a handful of parched corn. With the camp chores completed, they fell asleep.

November 20 brought more of the same, slogging through flooded, muddy fields and crawling over fallen trees and through thick underbrush. These horrible field conditions, the strain of the escape, and little food sapped the strength of the already worn-out men.

As the pair ventured on they heard a rustling and grunting sound of something rooting in the undergrowth. Slipping up behind some brush they could see several pigs. Loring looked at Flory. Flory looked back at Loring and licked his lips. Ham and bacon on the hoof. Loring grabbed a dead tree branch to be used as a club. Flory slowly stepped out from behind the brush, calling quietly to the potential dinner, "Come piggy-y-y, poor, nice piggy-y-y, poor hungry piggy-y-y, here's something nice for you."[4] Flory held out a small handful of the parched corn. He approached the nearest pig. In a soothing, cooing voice he tried to lure the pig toward the brush where Loring waited with the club. The pig could smell the corn and hesitantly approached Flory. Flory slowly backed away toward the brush. The pig followed.

Loring came down hard with the club! He missed the pig's head but badly injured its leg. The pig squealed, whirled about, and the chase was on. The injured pig ran for its life, darting in and out of the trees. Loring was right behind, swinging at it with his club, always just a half step off. On just three legs the pig made its escape and left Loring and Flory tired and with a bit less parched corn to call their own. All the men could do was move on.

28

Over the River and through the Woods

On November 24 the men enjoyed their Thanksgiving dinner of a handful of parched corn and were genuinely thankful for that as they approached a small town called Town Bluff. They crawled and crept from bush to bush, staying on the edge of town. With a good vantage point they could see men working in a sawmill on the banks of the Neches River.[1] Loring was sure that with a mill so close to the water there must be a boat nearby that they could commandeer. Floating down the river would save miles of wear on their tired and sore feet. Being ever so cautious, it took them a half day to creep closer to the river and the mill. From their hidden vantage point a dozen slaves could be seen working. As boats pulled up on the riverbank several slaves would tie them off and unload them. Huge rafts of timber were disassembled, and teams of horses were used to haul the logs up the landing to the mill. Throughout the afternoon Loring and Flory lay hidden as they listened to the Negro songs and watched the men work.

As the sun went down Loring leaped into action. Eyeing a boat moored on the riverbank, he headed straight for it. Keeping low and partially hidden in the brush along the bank, Loring crept to within thirty feet of a cabin. Inside the cabin the slaves were going about their business, waiting for supper, joking, and singing. Loring readied to spring aboard the boat as the sound of oars creaking and dipping in the water reached him. He looked out across the water and saw another boat headed right toward him. The boat pulled ashore only fifteen feet away.

Loring ducked, keeping his head down. Two white men stepped on shore and headed up the bank toward the cabin. This boat was closest, and Loring took advantage of the opportunity. In one motion he slipped into the boat and shoved off. He hastily grabbed the nearest oar and used it as a paddle while he sat in the bow of the boat. Moving quickly, before the owners might find their boat missing, Loring searched the riverbank for some sign of Flory. Not seeing any sign of him, Loring pulled the boat into the weeds along the bank. Flory had watched the entire situation unfold and shadowed Loring, waiting for him to pull ashore. As Loring pulled up Flory jumped in.

With Flory aboard, Loring put the oars in the oarlocks and pulled the boat out into the river. Once out in the middle Flory took his turn at the oars. With very little experience rowing Flory had difficulty maneuvering the boat in a straight line.[2] Loring gave him some instruction and with a little practice the colonel began to get the hang of it. Flory was a quick learner. With the added incentive of having their lives on the line, he found his rhythm. Flory straightened the boat out and they headed downriver.

The current was slow and the river wound back on itself. After thirty minutes of rowing they had made just several hundred yards of actual progress. They rowed to the east side of the river, climbed out, and scrambled up the bank. Exhausted from rowing, the hungry, sore men made camp on the east side of the Neches River.

29

Bear Swamp

The men were cold and wet. There was no sun, and the surrounding countryside was flooded. It had been the same for the previous ten days. It made no sense to continue to follow the Neches River. The men abandoned the boat and headed east. They slogged, waded, swam, and pulled themselves through some of the thickest undergrowth, canebrakes, and brambles imaginable. It was not only physically tiring but mentally draining. Unable to see more than a few feet ahead, they would occasionally pop into a small opening that held some stagnant pool of water. The water was murky and the depth was never known until the first step. Loring, in the lead, would at times disappear as he stepped into a hole. Reaching the opposite side, the process would begin again. But the men kept moving.

Flory was still suffering from a fever and was having some difficulty keeping up with Loring. As the men rested for a moment Loring scanned the sky for a glimpse of the sun to check their direction of travel. With no break in the clouds, they pushed on. Loring led and forced his way through some thick brush. As he bulled his way through the brambles he heard a huffing sound. When he parted the undergrowth he came face to face with a bear.

From five feet away they stared at each other for what seemed an eternity. The bear, equally surprised, popped his teeth, swapped ends, and took off in the opposite direction, parting the brush as if it were just tall grass on the prairie.[1] Stunned, Loring fell back into the waist-deep water and muck. He looked up. Flory was still staring in the direction that the bear had gone. Loring quipped, "Did you see that?" Flory deadpanned, "Well, it was hard to tell. I was eight feet away, but you had the best seat in the house."

With Flory's help Loring pulled himself up out of the muck. As the men contemplated their next move the sun shone through the clouds long enough for Loring to fix their location to avoid walking in circles. Ninety minutes later they broke out of the swamp and encountered a river. As they sat down to rest, Loring noticed several logs and other debris. He suggested to Flory that they make a raft. Searching about, the men gathered any material that would float. They threw together a small raft that would be capable of supporting the few belongings they had. Held together with blankets, belts, suspenders, and their canteen strap, it resembled a pile of flotsam.

Loring stuffed his knapsack with what was left and tied that to his head. They hauled the raft to the water's edge. Each man held onto the sides of the raft and kicked out into the swirling current. Flory almost immediately began to struggle. His muscles contracted and cramped as his energy was sapped by the cold water. Barely able to hang on, he told Loring he had no strength left. Loring implored him to hang on. He gave a few more kicks, just enough to propel them into slower-moving water closer to the opposite shore. Chilled completely through, with stiff legs and arms, neither man could stand. The naked men crawled out of the water and up the muddy bank onto a dry spot. The landscape had changed. The ground beyond was higher and consisted of oak and pine. They had reached the edge of the swamp.

Loring dismantled the raft as Flory rested. They quickly dressed and followed a path in an easterly direction as darkness and exhaustion caught up to them. They made camp and enjoyed a small fire, but food was scarce. With only a handful of parched corn each, it "was nothing more nor less than a slow process of starvation . . . rapidly sapping our live's foundation."[2] Because no real calories could be derived from the corn, their bodies suffered. The tramping through briers and brambles in the swamp had shredded their bodies and clothing. The combination made for quite a sight; gaunt drawn men clothed in tatters. Loring in particular suffered tremendously from his ill-fitting boots. With two more nails ripped off and blisters on top of blisters, his feet were raw. Mentally, Flory was nearing the end of his resolve. Loring was steadfast. He would escape to Union lines or die trying. It was that simple. Loring encouraged Flory by setting small goals and breaking down the journey into five-mile increments. He often reminded his partner that it was only five miles to the next road junction or just another hour to the next river crossing. They pushed on.

On November 25 the sky finally cleared. That night the men could clearly see the twinkle of the stars. Loring turned his face toward the heavens and found comfort in the constellations that had for many years been his road map to home and safe harbors.[3] He popped a few kernels of parched corn into his mouth, turned to Flory, and pointed toward the Big Dipper. Loring explained how to find the North Star by first locating this constellation. He instructed Flory to follow the handle to the ladle and imagine pouring some water from it. The water would flow right to the North Star. If the skies were partially obscured and there was only a crescent moon you could imagine a line between the two points all the way down to the horizon and that would show the way south. Flory looked up, munching on his parched corn. "You see," said Loring, "you are never really lost; the stars will always guide you home."

Flory smiled and thought of home as he inched closer to the fire. With the clear skies came a drop in temperature to below freezing. Their meager dinner completed, the men groaned as they struggled to their feet to continue on.

Ice formed on the rain-soaked ground. Two weeks of rain had even caused flooding on the high ground, with three to twelve inches of water. Loring led the way and broke the ice so Flory could save his strength. It was a tiring, grueling process. Each step required Loring to lift his leg above the ice and put his full weight on it to break it. As miserable as he was, Loring was thankful that the freezing water numbed his feet so he could no longer feel the blisters.

Following the heavens' starry guideposts, Loring confidently navigated across the countryside. The miles began to add up as they followed an old road. Loring suddenly stopped and Flory nearly walked into him. A river stood in their way. It was the Sabine River at Burr's Ferry Bridge. The remnants of old bridge pilings were barely visible just above the floodwaters. Two weeks previously the men could have easily skipped across without getting wet. Now they would have to carefully assess how to cross this obstacle. They stripped off their clothes and slid down into the water near the pilings. Searching about on the water's edge, they found a couple of boards. Combining this with a few other sticks they constructed a platform to place their clothes on, using their belts and suspenders to hold it together. They pushed this platform in front of them as they swam across. Reaching the opposite side the naked men were barely able to crawl up the bank, as the first stage of hypothermia set in. Shaking nearly uncontrollably, they helped each other to dress. They had made it to Louisiana.

Staggering on, they passed a roadside cottage as a clock inside struck 3:00 a.m. Completely spent, they moved off the road into the forest and found a thicket in which to conceal themselves. Flory attempted to build a fire but was shaking so badly he was unable to strike a match. Loring helped his friend and they managed to spark a small fire. Grateful for a handful of parched corn, they huddled next to the fire and recounted the close call at Bear Swamp and shared stories of home. Flory looked up and pointed out the North Star. Loring put his small penknife back in his pocket after quietly repairing his boots. As he lay down he too looked up at the stars. Drifting off to sleep, he thought, "Yes, my friend, that is the way home."

30

Confederate Potatoes

Loring and Flory had run out of cover. It was time for the men to face the South up close and personal. The men had traversed the swamps, forests, and rivers and they had no choice now but to continue on disguised as Confederate soldiers. They adjusted and improved their appearances as best they could. Flory cut the tattered reinforced knee patches from his trousers. Loring pulled the bottoms of his trousers out of the tops of his boots to hide his dilapidated footwear. They washed their faces and combed their matted, tangled hair with a pine cone.[1] After inspecting each other they each pinned in place a Lone Star badge, the final accoutrement to their disguise. They broke camp and struck out, heading south and trying to stay parallel to the river while hiding in plain sight.

It wasn't long before they were tested. In the front yard of a smallish cottage was a woman tending to a small garden. In a Southern drawl, Loring struck up a conversation with the woman with the intent of divining just exactly where they were. Loring tried not to arouse any suspicion as he asked how far away the Sabine River was. The woman stated she did not know and that she didn't "go round much."[2] She told Loring that perhaps the Browns would know, they were the next house down the road. Loring and Flory headed in the direction the woman pointed. Reaching the next house, the men encountered two more women. Loring again asked about the Sabine River, trying to make conversation. These ladies were better informed. They had traveled on the Sabine road previously but that was three miles back from where the men had just come. The ladies recommended that they head that way and inquire for specific directions from a Mr. Purcell. The men took the advice. With confidence in their disguises they backtracked with the goal of finding Mr. Purcell and perhaps a meal.

For two days the men had walked, stopping only briefly for a couple of hours' rest at a time. Loring's feet were badly blistered and Flory was still feverish, but this played in their favor. It was best to arrive at Mr. Purcell's just prior to dark, so the men walked slowly. Coming to a fork in the road the men wondered if they had gone the right way. Loring noticed a small board with faded writing on it nailed to a tree. The sign read, "To Ballou's Ferry 5 miles."[3] They could not believe their eyes. Using the wind, sun, and stars Loring's dead reckoning had brought them within five miles of their destination.

At dusk they arrived at Mr. Purcell's inn on the banks of the Sabine River at Ballou's Ferry. As they approached the inn they were met by Mr. Purcell, who immediately made it very clear that he had seen many suspicious men in the course of the war. He was wary.

Loring spoke first. "Me an him—that's Mr. Miller, there, has walked but 10 miles this whole day, but we's rid mos' all the way's far's Woodvill . . . . where we laid over for the flood to go off." Flory chimed in. "True, every word true." With a quick suggestion that they had passes, they manipulated the conversation away from the topic. There was a long pause as Purcell sized up the men and considered their story. Having made up his mind, Purcell simply asked, "Gentlemen, are you ready for supper?"[4] Loring and Flory tried to hide their excitement about an actual meal. It would be their first in nearly two weeks.

Dinner was incredible: cornbread, beans, and some pork; it was a feast. With full bellies the men retired to sit beside the fireplace and delighted in warming themselves next to the roaring fire. Loring led the conversation and heartily berated the Yankees at any chance. They traded stories with their host, skillfully avoiding any conversational piece that might lead back to them. During the conversation they ascertained the location of nearby rebel patrols and strongholds so they could avoid them. For the next two hours Henderson (Loring) and Miller (Flory), the fraudulent Confederates, honed their story.

Loring and Flory were comfortable when the sound of an approaching rider brought them to attention. The rider pulled up on horseback and inquired as to whether he could stable his horse and stay the night. Purcell obliged and the unidentified man took the horse to the barn. Flory took the opportunity to excuse himself for the night. He slipped out the door to the front porch, wrapped himself in his blanket, and lay down to sleep. Loring lingered a bit so as not to arouse suspicion. The unknown man came in from the barn. The two men nodded and acknowledged each other. Loring excused himself and joined Flory.

Flory was lying right next to the saddle, saddlebags, and other accoutrements that the man had placed on the porch before leading his horse to the stable. Being a resourceful fellow, Flory had quickly perused the contents of those bags for anything useful or edible. He quietly disclosed to Loring that the bags held a large quantity of corn and sweet potatoes but then corrected himself. They used to hold some sweet potatoes. "I have relieved that poor mule of 8 big, fat ones."[5] Loring grinned. Slumping to the floor, he fell into a deep sleep for the first time in fourteen days.

Early the next morning Purcell's other guest gathered his belongings lying next to Flory and headed to the barn to saddle up for the day. The saddle bags were quite a bit lighter. Flory knew this man would notice and that this had the potential to cause a serious issue. He told Loring he was heading out and would leave the lying to him and his silver tongue. Flory hightailed it out of sight just as the man discovered the thievery. "Landlord! Some of your g—d . . . niggers stole half my potatoes last night."[6]

Purcell responded with, "My people have all the potatoes they can eat. They are not that kind of nigger, anyhow!" The upset man lamented, "They are gone for all that; where are they? They were real beauties that I brought along to eat on the road, and there warnt but a few of them in the first place." The exchange became heated and tempers flared on both sides. Then Purcell interjected a comment that changed the direction of the ire entirely. "Perhaps those two soldiers can tell you something about them."[7]

Hearing the word *soldiers* caused the enraged man to change his demeanor. Suddenly the value and loss of the potatoes seemed less egregious. He was willing to let the whole incident go. After all, they were Confederate soldiers. The disgruntled man muttered something under his breath. He mounted his horse and spurred the animal into action down the road. Loring did not want to draw any more suspicion than had already come his way. As he moved to the table for breakfast he noticed Purcell waving to a boy outside. It was Purcell's fifteen-year-old son. With a knowing glance and nod of the head the boy communicated that he had found some of the potatoes wrapped in Loring's blanket. Without saying a word, Loring produced one of the silver dollars Flory had traded his buttons for.[8] He flipped it to Purcell and slid the rest of the leftover breakfast into his knapsack. As he skipped off the porch he winked at the boy and sailed down the road to join Flory.

Goodbye, Texas

L oring caught up to Flory a few hundred yards down the road. Readjusting their knapsacks, they slung them over their backs. They pushed on down the road. Loring looked at Flory with a renewed sense of energy. "Eastward, my friend." Flory turned around, faced west, and snapped a salute, "Goodbye Texas!" They had no intention of recrossing the Sabine River and ever setting foot in Texas again.

Loring looked up at the sun to determine their location and direction of travel. Pointing east, he looked at Flory and stated, "This way to Lake Charles City." Full of confidence from their overnight charade with Mr. Purcell, the men decided to continue on the road toward Niblett's Bluff. By avoiding the undergrowth and thick vegetation the men traveled the five miles to Niblett's Bluff before they knew it.[1] The town bustled with wartime business as the two men walked along the main street.

Unsure of where the road to Lake Charles City was, Loring stopped a slave and asked him to point out the road. The man was unable to help. The pair moved on into the center of the town. The street became more congested; there were people everywhere. Loring and Flory grew anxious as townspeople began to look at them. They were drawing too much attention. Still in need of directions, they reconsidered their current course and took a side street leading out of town. Reaching the edge of the town, they faced a flat and featureless prairie flooded in the lowest areas from the rain.

As the light faded and darkness fell Loring again looked to the heavens for guidance. "We turned to a star in the East, as it were the Star of Bethlehem, and while struggling along under its guidance we 'blessed our stars' for the light of its countenance."[2]

The temperature dropped and the flooded low-lying areas of the prairie began to ice over. Loring suffered tremendously as the ice sheets broke across his nearly fully exposed feet in the remnants of his boots. Exhausted, they found some dry ground about fifteen feet in diameter and made camp for the remainder of the night. For fear of being seen and with no wood anyway they did not build a fire. They pulled their threadbare blankets around themselves and, sitting back to back, they shivered and waited for morning.

Morning dawned. Flory poked Loring and pointed at a sight they had not seen in days. The sun was on the horizon in its full glory! The men stood and stretched as the sun climbed higher. Their spirits were lifted as their broken bodies soaked up the warmth. Loring determined their direction of travel. But they took their time. Like reptiles, they basked in the luxury of the sun as their cold, stiff legs and backs warmed and slowly loosened. The sun was fully above the horizon as both men surveyed the land around them. There was nothing but a sea of hummocks with skim ice in the lower areas. They pulled on their packs. Loring looked down at his raw feet. He took a moment. He reminded himself that in order to once again report for duty he must continue on. He prepared himself for the pain that would accompany wading through the ice-filled troughs, knowing that this would bring him one day closer to freedom.

32

Home Guard and Yankee Prisoners

Loring's feet were red with blood as he hobbled along. The men could walk for only thirty minutes at a time and then needed to rest as they followed a series of cattle trails eastward. After three hours of walking and wading they came to a ranch. Desperate for some food, they sidled up to the front of the house and encountered a man butchering a side of beef. They had not eaten in two days. The man looked up from his work and squared his shoulders toward Loring as blood dripped from the blade of his huge knife. Flory hung back as Loring moseyed up to the butcher. In a Southern drawl, Loring asked if they might be given something to eat. The butcher responded, "Something to eat? Yes seein's how you's sojers, Home Guards, eh?" Loring answered, "No! Not by a jug full. We prides ourselves on bein Reg'lars."[1] The butcher called for his wife and told her to prepare a meal for the men.

The men waited and watched the butcher at his craft. Loring kept up the conversation, trying to subtly ascertain the road to Lake Charles City. During the conversation the butcher mentioned he was the local law, a constable. Flory nearly flinched but caught himself when he heard this. Loring looked at Flory with steely eyes, reassuring him. Both men lavished the constable with praise, stressing the need for important and ethical men like him. With the conversation at an awkward lull, dinner was pronounced ready and the men concentrated on chewing and swallowing.

With the feast complete, they excused themselves and Loring asked for directions to the Lake Charles City road. The constable struggled to provide directions they could actually follow. Loring thanked the couple for their hospitality as Flory led the way down the road. Rounding a corner, Flory was dismayed to encounter yet another bayou that prevented them from easily continuing. The men exchanged knowing glances and began to comb through the tall grass for anything that might be used to float across the water. With luck on their side they found what appeared to be the constable's canoe. Loring commandeered the canoe in the name of the Federal navy. Jumping in and paddling across, both men were ecstatic to not have to cobble together some pile of wood that might or might not actually float.

Across the bayou they disembarked and headed out on the muddy prairie. Unable to find the road, they moved in an easterly direction, hoping to come across it. As they plodded along they noticed that they were never very far from the next farm or plantation. Carefully but confidently they moved across the prairie and through farm fields. Following a split-rail fence line, they found themselves staring at a huge field of sweet potatoes. There was one slave in the field, bent over and tending to some plants. Loring called out to the slave as he limped closer. When they were within earshot Loring commented that it was over a year since he and his companion had eaten a sweet potato. The Negro looked the men over and said something about how even though the men looked poorly he could not give them any food because it belonged to Mr. Morse, his master.

The Negro pointed Loring and Flory toward the big house where Morse, the owner, lived. Arriving at the steps of the big house, Loring was introduced to three women who stated clearly that Morse was not at home but was away on business. Loring was direct and asked if they could spare some food for two poor soldiers headed home to remount. The women gave what they could, "a pint of meal, and a spoonful of salt."[2] Loring asked if they might not have any sweet potatoes but the women told them to be on their way and not cause any trouble. Flory nodded his thanks and Loring asked for directions to the Lake Charles City road. The women had no knowledge of such a road but in an attempt to be helpful one of the women called for her teenage son to come and take these gentlemen around. The boy dutifully showed Loring and Flory the farm and surrounding fields.

During the tour the boy mentioned that several days previously he and others had seen two men skulking along the edge of the woods. It was raining heavily that day and the men came to the farmhouse seeking food. The young man's father, Mr. Morse, talked with them and discerned that they appeared confused and disoriented. He was sure that they were escaped Yankee prisoners on the run from Camp Groce. Loring spat on the ground. Those boys should be tarred and feathered. The young boy heartily agreed, saying he would like to have a chance to shoot one of them Yankees. Loring asked quizzically, "You said they were escaped from Camp Grocery?" "No," the boy retorted, "Camp Groce, up near Houston somewhere." Flory reached out and took hold of Loring's arm. "Let the boy continue his showing the farm." Loring made his Southern sympathies clear by suggesting that the boy join the Confederate army and come with them. The boy gulped and turned to continue the tour. Loring knew they needed to end this conversation and move on. He laid it on thick with the boy. "You see we'v had awful bad luck with drummer boys since we started out. One died er grief in our last ditch 'cause the yanks bust his drum. One was drounded, another was catured an' skinned alive an' cooked an' eat by the cannerbul yanks, an' two was blowed all to smithereens by yankee shells, an' the last one—well he froze from sleepin' rough-like in the trenches—an' the beauty of it all is they died young an' beloved. Golly: but they had lots er fun, an' just so may you; an' its just as easy as rollin' off a log."[3] The boy's mouth was agape, his eyes huge. In a single motion he said no and turned on his heels to leave, pointing in a general direction and saying, "That way to the road" as he skedaddled back home. The tour was over. Seven miles outside of Lake Charles City, the men camped for the night.

The next day the men rested and waited until 3:00 p.m. before heading toward Lake Charles City. They thought it prudent to approach the city as darkness was falling. Completely dependent on the generosity of others for food, they took full advantage of any possibility of securing a meal. Loring's feet were terribly painful and he picked up a walking stick to help steady him and take some of the pressure off his feet. The men slowly dragged themselves along the road. Loring turned to Flory and with a few words of encouragement told him they would take a break at the next house they came to. With dark upon them, Loring, under the guise of Mr. Henderson, strode up to the door of a ramshackle old home while Flory hid in the brush and waited. Loring knocked on the weather-beaten door and declared that he was a poor Confederate soldier. A woman opened the door. Loring, with cap in hand, asked if she could spare some rations for such a poorly soul. To Loring's surprise he was invited in. He was lavished with "cold fresh beef, sweet potatoes-hickory-nut size-corn bread, and bacon too of a quality not so over ripe as that of confederate hades."[4]

Loring sat down with the woman and her two young daughters and devoured what was placed in front of him as poor Flory waited in the bushes. The woman just sat and stared. The girls looked on wide-eyed with their mouths open as Loring gulped down the food. Looking up, Loring explained, "I have a brother in arms who is too ashamed of his raggedy appearance from battlefield service to his country to come in. Would you mind if I take just a few bites out to him?"[5] Without hesitating or waiting for a response, Loring pulled a cloth out of his pocket. He opened it up on the table and piled the remaining food onto it. He wrapped it up, tied the four corners together, and pushed back from the table all in one motion before the family realized what was happening. Still half chewing and swallowing, Loring thanked them for their hospitality and backed toward the door. The woman and her girls stood speechless. Loring turned and waved as he reached the gate. Flory popped out from behind a tree and Loring presented him with his share of the meal, all nicely wrapped.

33

Old Friends?

Flory ate while they walked and enjoyed the hospitality of the most recent Southern family to contribute to their mobile pantry. Rounding a corner, Loring pointed to a sign at the fork in the road nailed to a tree, which read, "Glendenning's Ferry 5 Miles."[1] Severely hobbled, it took them over two hours to cover the distance. Loring's feet were in terrible shape and Flory was still feverish. Just prior to dark they arrived at the river landing and briefly surveyed the area in the waning light. They decided the best course of action was the simplest. Loring called out to the opposite riverbank and announced that they were Confederate soldiers who required passage across. The response came a few minutes later as a small boat rowed into sight to pick them up.

Aboard and underway, the trip across the river took only a few minutes. As the oarsman put his back into it Loring inquired as to how far they were from Vermillion (present-day Lafayette) and was Mr. Glendenning on the premises? Before the oarsman could answer Loring caught a glimpse of a much larger ship in the faint glint of light coming off the water. As the small rowboat glided past the moored ship Loring asked what it was. The oarsman responded, "The *Granite City*." Both men barely hid their amazement. Loring inquired further. "The *Granite City*! . . . Where did she come from?" The oarsman explained that the ship had been captured at Calcasieu Pass and had been brought upriver to "keep the Yankees from stealin' ere back."[2] Loring discreetly eyed Flory at the news. They were truly in the midst of the lion's den.

The rowboat slid to a stop on the opposite shore. Loring and Flory got out of the boat, still amazed that the *Granite City* lay anchored in the river. Loring cast one final glance upriver at the ship and wondered if the *Wave* still lay in its watery grave. He turned to follow Flory up the landing but froze in his tracks as a boy barely in his teens greeted the men with a revolver pointed directly at them. Flory swallowed hard and Loring was stunned but quickly came to his senses and pronounced, "Whoa there, son, no need to be drawin' a bead on a couple of Confederates headed home to remount." With a nod from the oarsman the boy lowered the gun and led the men up the bank to the home of the proprietor of Glendenning's Ferry. Mr. Glendenning himself greeted them at the top.

Loring took Glendenning's hand and firmly shook it with the confidence and familiarity that only a Southern soldier would have. He mentioned that the young man there would someday make a fine sentry. Wasting no more time, Loring launched into a monologue. "Mr. Glendenning! I hardly recognized you. How are you? I'm awful glad to see you. I was not sure if we would find you here or if you had been conscripted into the army as so many others have been. You seem to have escaped it all." Loring took a breath and sized up Glendenning's reaction to him before continuing. "You do remember me, don't you? Well, it would not surprise me if you didn't. It has been, let's see, nearly five years ago that I made several crossings here. I was on my way to my old friend Morse's to trade a horse." Glendenning, unsure of Loring's identity, hesitantly nodded.

Loring pointed over his shoulder at Flory. "That there is Miller and I am Henderson of the firm Miller and Henderson, livestock dealers over on the Teche River.[3] I can't blame you for not recognizing me. Five years will change a man, especially when three of those years have been in the field fightin' Yankees." The words tumbled from Loring's lips as smooth as only practice could make them, when one's life depends on it. His forehead furrowed, Glendenning thought for a moment, trying to recall Mr. Henderson. Flory saw his opportunity. He stepped forward, extended his hand to Glendenning, and introduced himself as Mr. Miller, "Glad to make your acquaintance." With a hearty handshake they solidified their bond of Southern brotherhood.

Glendenning seemed to relax and was satisfied with Loring's story that they had known each other years previously. As the men walked toward the house, Glendenning explained that he was doing his part in support of the South as part of the Home Guard along with his two sons. Hearing this, Flory shot a look at Loring. Loring told Glendenning that they had papers and then quickly changed the topic as he cursed the Yankees. Glendenning invited the men to stay the night and have dinner with him. In the morning they could share a ride in his wagon for ten miles before they would have to part ways. Accepting the invitation, Loring and Flory walked into the pit of vipers.

After a sumptuous dinner Glendenning made a side comment as the men excused themselves: "It would be in your best interest to head into Opelousas tomorrow to have your passes signed by the commanding officer. I wouldn't want you to have a run in with some of the local boys of the home guard."[4] Both men nodded as they spread out on the floor to sleep. With full bellies, they slept soundly, knowing that the morning would bring some difficult decisions.

The first of December broke cold and concerning on the eighteenth day of the escape. The Glendenning family was up and the business of the day had already begun before Loring and Flory stirred. Wagons were being brought up and loaded. The men faced a difficult situation to avoid traveling into town to have their passes signed. Loring and Flory quietly ate breakfast and pondered their dilemma.

Suddenly Loring looked up from his meal and turned to Flory. "Oh, Mr. Miller, I have plum forgot all about the passes being signed! If we go all the way in to Opelousas we will miss that ten-mile ride. You know it's a much better deal to ride for free than wear ourselves out walking all that way. If it were up to me I would rather run the risk of those local Home Guard boys than miss out on that ride." Flory agreed and added, "Yes, Mr. Henderson, I agree. You know how your knee gives you trouble since being shot by them damn Yankees." Loring called over to Glendenning, who had overheard the conversation. "What do you say, Mr. Glendenning? We will leave the decision in your hands." Flory's eyes widened as he heard this.

Glendenning thought out loud. "You may not see any Home Guard and once you are twenty miles from here you would be as safe as if you were in my own home." Loring saw the opening and took full advantage of it, accepting the decision. Glendenning then threw one more wrench in the works. "Of course you never know. You might run across Colonel Brough, commander of the home guard. He lives in Vermillion. He is there visiting family and is expected back shortly."[5] Loring and Flory nodded in acknowledgement.

With breakfast consumed and the remaining cornbread stowed for later consumption, Loring paid Glendenning a silver dollar and Flory purchased some tobacco for another dollar. With packs slung over one shoulder the pair stepped out into the yard. Slaves loaded the final sacks of goods into the wagons as the men climbed aboard. Loring and Flory were thankful for the ride and as the mules leaned into their halters they couldn't help but wonder what dangers the road ahead held.

34

Your Passes or Your Life!

Loring and Flory jumped off the wagon train at a split in the rutted road. They were anxious to leave the area in which the Home Guard might be patrolling and avoid an encounter with Colonel Brough. A quarter mile down the road was an old man leaning up against a rickety fence in front of his equally rickety old house. The old man stared at Loring and Flory as they approached. Loring called out to the man. "Hello. Mister man! How de do? How far to Welsh's? Has y'r got anything we fellers can eat?"[1] The man was taken aback by Loring's forwardness. The old man retorted that he had nothing cooked but he did have some beef and potatoes in the cellar. They could have some of it if they wanted, seeing as they looked so poorly.

Tired, both men sat down in the grass in the old man's yard. Loring rubbed his lame hip. A shriveled-up old woman appeared from around the corner of the house. Her apron held several large potatoes and over her right shoulder was an entire side of beef ribs. She dropped the ribs on the fence and emptied her apron. The men could not believe their luck. The potatoes disappeared into their knapsacks. In a hurry Loring asked the old man if he could cut up the ribs into a couple of sections. The old man obliged. The men unrolled their blankets, slid the ribs in, and rolled them back up. Time was pressing and both men wanted to continue. Flory helped Loring adjust his knapsack and thanked the old man and his wife for their hospitality. The old man told the men they didn't need to be in such a hurry, they were among friends of the cause.

Loring and Flory moved toward the gate as the old man commented about the Home Guard in the area. He kept talking and started to follow them. Loring nodded and waved over his shoulder as he followed Flory out the gate. The old man, now suspicious and talking still louder, identified himself as a sergeant of the Home Guard.[2] He told the men to stop and show him their papers. Flory stopped suddenly. Loring looking back over his shoulder at the old man walked right into Flory's back. Loring turned completely to face the sergeant and said, "Yes, of course. We have shown our papers to many people."

Knowing that they must sell their ruse fully, the two men began to dig in their packs in search of the forged passes. While rummaging around they also began to flatter the man, calling him captain, much to his pleasure. Finally pulling the scraps of papers from their packs and presenting them to the Home Guard sergeant, they awaited the verdict. After studying the passes, the sergeant announced, "They are all right!" Henderson (Loring) and Miller (Flory) confirmed that of course they were fine and those who had previously inspected the papers had found them to be fine as well.

With this the sergeant offered an apology for making the men produce the papers. Loring and Flory scoffed at the necessity. "Oh, spare yourself apologies, you are a reliable soldier. You deserve well of the country for so faithfully performing yours. In fact your faithfulness is only exceeded by your generosity, and when we come back to the City we shall recommend that Colonel Brough promote you to lieutenant-by brevet."[3] With this Loring offered one final piece of flattery and asked if the sergeant would sign their passes to further endorse them. The sergeant thought about this for a moment and again stated that the passes were just fine and that would not be necessary. With the repartee completed, Loring and Flory said their good-byes and again headed back down the long road toward freedom.

Several hundred yards down the road their hunger pains would no longer allow them to ignore the veritable feast in their packs. Sliding off the road into the brush, they made a small fire to roast the potatoes and cook the ribs. They devoured the potatoes and barely edible ribs in mere minutes and laid up to ruminate before beginning the trek anew. With their food well digested they continued on the road and late that night came to another bayou. In what had become customary fashion when presented with such an obstacle the men searched about for some way to cross. Finding a small boat, they rowed across the bayou near Lacassine.[4]

Stumbling about in the dark, the two men fell upon a home with a faint light in the window. While attempting to discreetly peek inside they were quickly discovered. Mr. Welsh, with shotgun in hand, met Loring at the door. Loring immediately divulged that they were Confederates on their way home to remount. Welsh, a steadfast secessionist, invited the men in and introduced them to Mrs. Welsh and their two daughters, who were seated near the fire carding cotton.[5] With introductions made Loring and Flory, now in their practiced roles of Henderson and Miller, told stories of the battlefield and generally derided the Yankees, thus gaining the confidence of their hosts. Food was shared and many stories were exchanged as the evening wore on. The family said good night and offered a bed to the weary men. It was the first bed that either man had slept in in nearly a year. While at first this was a luxury, neither man found it comfortable, and they eventually ended up on the floor.

Welsh's generosity had limits, and the following morning he required Loring and Flory to pay one dollar each for the accommodations and food. Loring explained that they were quite poorly and being soldiers of the same sympathetic cause they would give them their thanks and be on their way. Welsh insisted they pay and emphasized his seriousness by taking a step closer to his shotgun propped up in the corner. Flory produced the final two silver dollars he had bartered for with the gold buttons from his officer's coat while still in Camp Groce. With their knapsacks full of cornbread and scraps of bacon they faced the uncertainty of the nineteenth day of their trek.

Only a mile into the morning's walk, Loring saw a man skulking toward them and pointed him out to Flory.[6] It was unclear who the man was. Flory suggested they move away and give this man some room to pass. Loring stated they needed to keep up appearances as Confederates headed home and must remain confident. As they moved closer they recognized the man as another Confederate soldier. He too was wearing ragged clothing and his hollow eyes and sallow cheeks told a story of deprivation without a word being exchanged. The stranger seemed suspicious and very tense. They asked no questions of him, and he seemed disoriented and not very knowledgeable about the area. Loring and Flory postulated that perhaps he was a deserter. The three men eyeballed each other. The stranger put up his hands with palms facing Loring and Flory in a gesture meaning do not come any closer. Silently they agreed, "You leave us alone an' we will you." The stranger looked up the road and then back down, seemingly unsure of which way to go. He left the road and shuffled off into the brush. Trudging onward across the flat expanses still flooded from rain, Loring and Flory reached a crossroad that seemed to head in the right direction so they followed it.

After several hours of painful limping along and more frequent stops to rest, they spotted a small, run-down cabin along the road. It appeared abandoned. The shutters hung at odd angles, the front door was ajar, the roof sagged and was missing several shingles, and there was no smoke coming from the crumbling chimney. But as they closed the distance it became apparent that it was indeed inhabited, as small voices could be heard coming from inside the hovel. Taking advantage of any opportunity that came their way, the men inquired for a meal. Loring announced their presence and was met at the door by a small child, perhaps four or five years old. The child looked up at the men with a dirty face and ran back inside, yelling, "Mama, Mama there are soldiers here!" A very tired and worn-looking woman came to the door holding another child who looked to be no more than two years old. Loring introduced himself and asked if she could spare some food for two poorly Confederate soldiers. The woman beckoned them in and told them to sit at the table. Loring pulled the door closed behind them.

The interior of the cabin was dank and nearly as bad as the outside. In the corner near the cold fireplace lay some filthy ticking with a few blankets on it. There was no firewood and no furniture other than the table. Loring kept up a conversation as he moved toward the table. Looking down, he saw that there were no chairs but a couple of stumps with a board between them. He and Flory sat down on this crude bench and were accompanied by a third child about six years old. The woman explained that her husband was off fighting Yankees and that she had not heard from him in over a year. The woman produced two small, wrinkled potatoes for the men. The meal was spare but both men were glad to have it. Clearly this woman was struggling to feed herself and her children. Loring pondered the deprivation that so many were feeling during this time of strife. The men ate in silence as the woman and children watched. The men stood and offered their thanks for the meal as Flory opened the cabin door. The cold and damp rushed in and brought them back to their own stark reality.

It had started to rain. Bracing themselves for a miserable walk, they peered down the road and spotted a wagon and carriage approaching. Attempting to avoid any encounters with the Home Guard or the infamous Colonel Brough, Loring led the way along a side road to avoid the oncoming strangers. The side road was undulating but provided drier footing up out of the low-lying water flooding the main road. They took several additional forked side branches and seemed to lose the oncoming wagons.

The rain fell steadily as Loring and Flory walked up a small rise in the road. Flory commented to Loring that they must have gotten around the wagons. As the men reached the crest in the road a wagon drawn by two horses suddenly appeared. The driver hauled back on the reins. The horses skidded to a stop less than twenty feet away from Loring and Flory! The undulating ground had hid the wagons and the men in the swales and the wet ground and mud had softened the hoofbeats of the horses. Neither party was aware of the other until they were nearly on top of each other. The driver of the carriage yelled out "Halt!" The man seated next to the driver stood up and in a commanding, staccato voice pointed his revolver at Loring and roared, "Your passes! Or your lives!"[7] It was Colonel Brough. Flory jumped, exclaiming, "Great Napoleon!" Loring turned and yelled, "Good Gawd, man!"

Staring up at the colonel they quickly searched through their knapsacks, keeping one eye on the revolver. The two soldiers in the back of the wagon now leveled their muskets at them. They handed their passes to the driver, who gave them to the colonel. Colonel Brough glanced at the passes and barked, "These are not correct. Do you live in Vermillion?" Flory (Miller) spoke up. He was familiar with the area since his regiment had passed through the previous year. "No! I don't exactly live there but have an Aunt who does, and when I visit there I make her house my headquarters." Colonel Brough inquired as to who he was referring to. Flory quickly and confidently stated her last name was Morse. Brough interrogated further, "Has she relatives in the Army?" Flory (Miller) responded, "She has a son."

Colonel Brough turned his attention away from that line of questioning, pointed the revolver at Loring, and demanded, "And where do you live?" Loring (Henderson), without blinking an eye, retorted, "I live at St. Martins, over on the Teche." Brough continued, "Who do you know there?" Loring responded in a cheeky way, "Oh, I know lots er people." With the demeanor of a man who is not to be trifled with Brough barked back, "Who!?" Loring began to get his dander up. "Well, my best friend is Johnson, George Johnson." Brough: "His occupation?" Loring: "He's a carpenter." Colonel Brough thought for a moment, trying to connect the name with a face that he knew. "Seems to me I don't know any George Johnson." Loring: "Perhaps you don't. All the same to you." Flory (Miller) jumped into the fray and redirected the conversation away from the inquisition about those they knew.

Colonel Brough turned his attention back to the passes. Pointing to them, he again stated they were incorrect. "Well I don't see how you got along with these passes. They are not correct." Loring declared, "We know that as well as you do. So did the officer that issued them, 'cause he said they needed the signiter of General Walker, but, said he, we can't wait for it on account of orders to start for Shreveport with as little delay as possible." Brough glared at the men. "Shall I tell you who I think you are? . . . I think you are a couple of Yankees-trying-to-escape-from Camp Tyler." Flory swallowed hard. Loring squared his shoulders and his hands curled into fists as he thought of the past nineteen days of suffering through hundreds of miles of swamps, bayous, water, and ice, with little food. He was not going to let all of their sacrifice come to an end like this.

Loring could not hold back; he took one step forward and let loose a tirade. "That's your opinion, is it? I tell you we's Confederates. Seems to me that's carrying your little joke too far and if twarnt for that big gun we would'nt be answerin impudent questions! Yankees-s-s. Ye-an-kees-s-s, eh! Hain't been to the front; have ye? Hai'nt seen many Yankees, nor many Confederate soldiers neither, cep'n home guards an' sech, or you'd er knowed Yankees wear good close, not like our rags. These Confederate rags is somethin' to be proud of. I spose your not Yankees or you wouldn't be cavortin' around in a carriage with a big gun botherin folks as is tryin to mind their business, peacable like. Here we's been a fitin' Yankees pretty nigh 4-year just for the fun er killin' um, without pay an a'most starved to death; an now we's called Yankees-s-s-s ourselves. I say it's goin' a little too far."

Colonel Brough was taken aback. Flory was stunned. If he hadn't been in the same prison with Loring even he would have been convinced Loring was a real Johnny Reb. Loring's verbal attack had the required effect. The tenor of the conversation changed from accusatory to one of acknowledgment. Colonel Brough sat down and lowered the revolver. He looked at the passes again and reiterated that they did not look right. How could these men have gotten this far with them? Loring and Flory defiantly looked him in the eye. Colonel Brough held out the papers. Loring snatched them from him. Colonel Brough mumbled under his breath, "Anyhow I don't-see-how-you-got-along-with-them." Taking advantage of the change in the colonel's demeanor, they moved past the wagon. The two soldiers in the back lowered their guns. Loring and Flory headed down the road as Loring called out over his shoulder, "We do . . .'cause we had no trouble."

They limped along as quickly as they could until they were out of sight of the colonel. Only fifteen minutes later, as the men began to relax and find their stride, another carriage with several fine women and men came into sight and reined to a halt. Flory bristled as Loring prepared for another verbal joust. The driver of the carriage tipped his hat to the men and exchanged pleasantries, stating, "You must be Confederate soldiers." The driver inquired whether they had seen any carriages or wagons earlier in the day. Loring acknowledged that indeed they were Confederate soldiers and they had not that long ago seen a wagon, one of the occupants of which was none other than Colonel Brough. The gentlemen seated next to the driver affirmed that indeed that was whom they were looking to intercept. Loring said to the gentleman, "As you are the colonel's friend it will give us much pleasure to make your acquaintance."[8] The man responded that he was Judge Mouton. Loring inquired further and extracted that this man was the brother of Governor Mouton of Louisiana. As the conversation concluded a Negro on a mule passed the group on the road.

Loring and Flory, still reeling from their encounters with Colonel Brough and the brother of Governor Mouton, shuffled off down the road. Only three hundred yards farther along Loring and Flory found a dirty old sack in the middle of the road. Groaning as he bent down to further inspect it, Loring found it held a cornucopia of food that could have been left only by an angel in disguise. Opening the bag they saw "sweet potatoes, cooked, small pieces of fresh beef . . . chunks of cornbread, which bore close relation to diamonds, both in value and density."[9] The old slave on the mule that passed by must have dropped it. For Loring and Flory it was a feast.

35

Where Is My Penknife?

Flory looked at Loring and with a smile pointed to the landing as the pair came into view of the Mermentau Ferry crossing.[1] The ferry itself was on the opposite bank and Loring hailed the captain to come across for them. The ferry seemed to take a long time and struggled to cross the river. As it pulled into shore it was clear the usual ferrymen had been replaced with Home Guard members who did not know how to operate the ferry proficiently.

Loring and Flory boarded the ferry and quickly noted they were among some dangerous and suspicious men. The man seemingly in charge was drinking heavily and swearing about their current situation. Alongside this man was an Indian who was silent but had an air of the desperate about him. The captain kept up a constant monologue during the crossing. Loring and Flory listened and occasionally nodded while avoiding being drawn into any discussion that could prove ill advised.

The ferryman commented on Loring's terrible condition and ragged appearance several times. He asked both men why they would fight for a country that would treat them with such disdain. In the next breath he added that for a half dollar each they could have a long draw on his bottle. It would fix any ailments they might be suffering. Loring told the ferryman that they had no money for drink nor any for the passage across the river. For good measure Loring added, "Our old friend, Colonel Brough, told us that soldiers traveled free everywhere."[2] The ferryman retorted that he did not charge soldiers for the crossing.

In a guarded tone Loring mentioned that they were headed toward Acadia and he wanted to clarify what road they needed to take. The Indian suddenly sat up and then standing sidled over toward the two men. He leaned in close. Loring could smell whiskey on the man's breath. "Well, friend, that's not the way you want to go. You want to make sure to stay to the right when the road forks." The

Indian was suddenly quite concerned with their safety and wanted to make sure they were headed the right way. Loring looked at Flory and knew what he was thinking. Judge Mouton had expressly stated that they needed to bear to the left after the Mermentau ferry and that staying to the right could put them in harm's way. Loring and Flory realized that they were being set up. They didn't want to tip their hand and cause a problem while still mid-river. They feigned interest in what was being said and asked for further clarification that they should continue on the right fork. The Indian nodded and stumbled back to his perch with an evil grin spreading across his face. He glanced sideways at one of the other ferrymen.

As the ferry pulled in to shore Loring and Flory quickly disembarked. They headed up the bank, eager to put some distance between themselves and these locals. As they rounded a bend and moved out of sight of the ferry landing they jumped into the brush to catch their breath and make some decisions. Both men agreed they needed to avoid the right fork and move quickly. Loring was in midsentence when Flory's head snapped about and he looked down the road where they had just come from. The sound of hoofbeats could be heard rapidly approaching. Both men pushed deeper into the brush. From seemingly nowhere a rider on horseback came galloping from around the corner.[3] It was the Indian! Holding a double-barreled shotgun across his lap, he spurred the horse down the right fork in the road, past Loring and Flory. Not even aware he had been holding his breath, Flory let out a long sigh and laid back in the brush as the Indian disappeared down the right fork in the road. He looked over at Loring. They would wait until dark before continuing on.

As darkness descended Loring and Flory struck out down the road. They slipped past several small shacks along the road but it took twice as long as usual to travel ten miles unmolested due to their pitiful physical condition. As the night wore on the weather again turned, the temperature dropped, and it began to rain. The men were exhausted, hungry, and sore. Loring's feet were blistered and bloody. Flory was stiff and feverish. Under what was left of the enameled cloth they "crouched and shivered in wretchedness."[4] Loring put a reassuring arm around his companion, saying,

"Buck up, we are very close now. Soon we will be able to report for duty." Flory stared at the half a handful of parched corn that was supper and shook his head, only able to muster a slight nod.

Dawn and the light of day revealed a great expanse of open fields. There was no concealment going forward. The men had covered twenty miles and were nearly outside of the Home Guard's range. Nearby they could see a small farm. Loring wondered aloud to Flory if that might hold their next meal. As Flory responded three slaves appeared at the edge of the field and drew near. Loring asked these men who the owner of the farm was and if he would be generous enough to give them something to eat.

The owner was a Cajun, the slaves said, and he was a kind man who would probably offer them some food. Wasting no time, Loring and Flory headed across the field toward the house. The field proved to be a formidable foe with the mud a foot deep. Loring suffered dearly while crossing the field. With each step, in his weakened condition and with a lame hip, he had to use his hands to pull his feet free from the boot-sucking mud. By the time they reached the house each man had five pounds of mud caked on his boots.

Arriving at the gate to the farmhouse Flory called out to announce their presence. The door to the house opened. The men were greeted by the Cajun, his wife, and several children with a warm welcome and an offer to pull up a chair near the fire.[5] Stamping the mud off on the porch steps, they entered the modest home and were each handed a tin cup of fresh steaming coffee, the likes of which they had not had in many months. Moving farther inside, both men were drawn to the fire like moths to a gas light. Standing next to the fire, steam began to emanate from their ragged clothing.

Loring fell into a practiced dialogue, reassuring their hosts that they were indeed Confederate soldiers heading home to remount and then rejoin their units. Flory followed suit. After gobbling up the few scraps of bacon and cornbread offered Loring stripped his wet clothes off and wrapped himself in his only blanket. He laid his clothes near the fire to dry. His boots had taken a horrible beating during the previous night's twenty-mile race and needed some repair. He reached into his knapsack to retrieve his sewing kit. It was gone. Loring remembered the previous day's encoun-

Where Is My Penknife?

ter. He and Flory had left their packs unattended in an adjacent room to enjoy a meal. This must have been when the sewing kit had been pocketed by some irksome person. His boots were in dire need of repair and Loring prevailed upon his hosts, asking if they could spare a needle and thread.

The Cajun gave Loring a large needle used to sew sackcloth and a long piece of candlewick for thread. Loring pulled his pocket-knife from his trousers near the fire, cut the wick to length, and laid the knife down, focusing on the sewing. Ready to cut another length of wick, he reached for the knife. It too was now missing. As he glanced about the room, several of the children looked up at Loring and then quickly averted their eyes to avoid his stares. Loring gently interrogated the child nearest to him. The boy sheepishly confessed that the knife may have ended up outside and he would go get it. With the knife retrieved and in hand, Loring finished the repairs to his boots.

Fully dressed in his dry clothes, Loring winced as he painfully slid his bloody feet into what was left of his boots. The Cajun could not help but notice the terrible condition of Loring's feet and commented, "Long walk, eh?" Flory looked out a window and casually mentioned that it was raining again. Loring winked at Flory and kept the conversation going, thinking to himself that there might be another meal if they extended their stay. At the very least they could avoid the weather a bit longer. Loring looked out the window and commented to no one in particular that it was nearly noon. The men were invited to another meal. Now they were out of excuses. They would need to leave or arouse suspicion as to their actual identities. With the meal over they picked up their belongings, slipped their knapsacks over their shoulders, and thanked their hosts.[6]

Marching down the road, Flory spotted a string of wagons a mile in the distance. Loring calculated that if they angled toward the line they could intercept the wagons and ask for a ride. Cutting across the muddy fields only slowed their progress and they missed the wagon train. As luck would have it one last wagon had straggled behind. Hobbling along the road as quickly as they could, they caught up to the wagon, which was driven by a slave. Loring asked the man for a ride but was told that only his master could give permission for them to do so. The wagon train had slowed and so the men hustled to the next wagon in line. They found a white driver and asked for a ride. The man slowed just enough for Flory to jump on. Loring struggled to keep up and reached out to Flory. Flory grasped Loring's arm and hauled him on board. Seated in the back of the wagon, Loring inquired as to the nature of the wagon train. The driver explained it was a "Confederate Government train bound for the New Iberia salt mines."[7]

Loring rubbed his sore legs and Flory smiled as they enjoyed the relative comfort of the ride. As the day drew to a close the wagon train slowed as the mud deepened and the wagons bogged down, becoming mired in the mud. The wagon master halted the column. He decided to wait until the next morning to continue. Loring and Flory took their cue and exited. They were now only seven miles from Vermillion.

The night was cloudy with no visible stars to help guide the men. Loring followed his nose and led the pair in a general direction of travel. Trying to conserve energy and not walk in circles, they searched for a house to ask for directions. Set back from what they assumed was the road Loring saw the faint glow of a candle through a shuttered window. Loring pounded on the door. This produced a sour response from inside. "What do you want?" Loring responded, "I want the road to Vermillion." Inside the house footfalls could be heard slowly approaching the door. The door squeaked open just enough to allow the muzzle of a shotgun to protrude.

Behind the barrel the eye of the inhabitant surveyed the men standing on the doorstep. Loring assured the man it was just two Confederate soldiers looking for the road to Vermillion. Deciding that was the case, the man stepped out from behind the door. He leveled the gun at Loring's chest and said, "Look out, there! What are you about?"[8] Loring very calmly reiterated they were looking for the road that would lead them to Vermillion. The man told them to follow the bayou till they came to the bridge and that's the road. He took two steps backward inside the house, loudly closed the door, and locked it.

The men followed the bayou for an hour until they came to a bridge. Flory suddenly grabbed Loring by the arm. "Ah! This is the Opelousas road! We must be near Vermillion. Now I know where I am."[9] Loring was jubilant. "All right! You may take the helm! I resign." With Flory in the lead they reached the outer limits of Vermillion by midnight. Flory suggested it would be best if they skirted the town. Loring had not seen Flory this energetic since the first few days of the escape. But their adrenaline-induced energy was soon sapped. Reaching the opposite side of the town they found the first dry spot, dropped down, and fell asleep.

36

The Last Toenail

With many people going about their business on a Sunday morning, the sounds of a large city coming alive reached the ears of Loring and Flory as they awoke. Neither man realized just how close to the edge of the city they had spent the night. They moved deeper into the woods to better conceal themselves while they surveyed their surroundings. The general bustle associated with a larger population reminded the men that civilization was now near and the dangers associated with it were increasing.

Loring jokingly told Flory he should go into town and pay a visit to his Auntie Morse, the one he had conjured up when confronted by Colonel Brough. Flory told Loring that wasn't funny. He explained that he had ridden with General Banks through the area and had liberated forty wagonloads of food from the city.[1] Flory was sure that if Auntie Morse ever saw him again she would turn him over to the rebel authorities or shoot him on sight. Hearing this, Loring reconsidered. They were too close to freedom to take any unnecessary risks. They devised a strategy to see them through to Union lines and freedom.

Loring calculated that they needed enough food for four days to cover the final eighty miles to freedom. If they covered twenty miles each night and if their legs did not give out they could make it. But both men were suffering and their bodies were falling apart, literally. The men readied their belongings to press on to the river.

Nearly a year before Flory and the Forty-Sixth Indiana Regiment had crossed the Vermillion River over the bridge at this exact point. The bridge was now gone due to flooding. The men would need to find another way to cross the Vermillion. At the edge of the woods they crawled on hands and knees for a quarter mile. They reached some brush at the bank of the river and searched for some way to cross it. Loring found an old boat but it had a six-inch hole in the stern.[2] He studied the wreck. They would have to make do. They could use it as a raft and swim it across. They put their belongings inside and struggled to haul the boat a short distance to the water. They stripped naked and shoved the boat into the current, hanging onto the sides of the weathered hull. They waded out into the frigid river, both men gasping as the cold water took their breath away. The boat quickly took on water through the hole as the two men kicked and clawed their way across.

Within a minute Flory yelled to Loring that he couldn't hang onto the boat much longer. The freezing water sapped the men's strength and chilled them to their core. The boat was sinking fast. Flory hung on with both hands but was barely able to kick. Loring yelled to hang on as they were nearly across. Flory's head slipped under and his grip on the boat loosened. Loring gave two more tremendous kicks and the boat, half full of water, slid into the shallows. He helped Flory move toward shore. Neither man was able to stand. They struggled, stumbled, and crawled through the cold, thick muck up the slick riverbank.

Shivering and shaking uncontrollably, they attempted to dry off, using their blankets as towels. Fully dressed, Loring reached for his boots. He looked at his blistered, disfigured feet and the scraps of leather that were his boots. He plucked off the final toenail dangling from his foot, dressed his blisters, and prepared for the night's twenty-mile hike.[3] Loring helped Flory to his feet and the men moved on.

The men had walked seventeen miles in nine hours when in the predawn Loring suffered from the contraction of his hamstrings. Flory grabbed Loring around the hip to help support him and they continued. As the sun peeked over the horizon neither man could move without the help of the other. Fearful that if they sat down they would not be able to stand up again, they rested frequently by leaning against fence rails or convenient trees. Reaching their goal of twenty miles, Loring and Flory crawled into the brambles along the road, made a small fire, and tried to rest.

Loring stared at his boots. They were beyond repair. He started to consider how to make a pair of moccasins from the materials in his knapsack but exhaustion overtook him.[4]

The men were completely played out and slept through most of the day. Loring woke just as the sun was dropping on the horizon. He hurriedly put his skills to work constructing a pair of moccasins from the enameled cloth previously used for a shelter. The moccasins were similar in design to those that Loring had made for de Doe. He rolled up the scraps of the boots and tucked them away in his knapsack as a keepsake. Loring and Flory ate the last of their rations: one potato, a few small chunks of cornbread, and the remnants of some bacon. As the sun set, the men took to the road. They needed to cover twenty miles before the dawn of the new day.

The painful miles slowly crept by. The men were so tired that they were nearly asleep as they walked. As they approached the outskirts of New Iberia Loring thought he heard some horses approaching. Slowly turning to look over his shoulder, he saw the silhouette of riders and hissed at Flory that men on horses were coming their way. Loring slid off the road into the brush. This did not immediately register with Flory. He reacted slowly and fell off the road into some tall grass. Flory heard the horsemen remark about a silhouette on the road, saying, "There goes a fine hog!"[5] It was a close call.

Loring and Flory dragged themselves back up onto the road. The miles slowly piled up as the men struggled to maintain their will to move on. Softly singing "John Brown's Body" and "Home Sweet Home" to themselves, they buoyed their spirits. With the final verse of "The Star Spangled Banner" the men reached the outskirts of Jeanerette.

Loring's hamstrings tightened up again and he could not fully extend his legs as he walked. Flory was hunched over under the weight of his knapsack. He took out his blanket and discarded it to reduce the weight. The men leaned on each other as they continued down the road. At daybreak, unable to go any farther, the weakened men slid down the back side of a railroad embankment and laid down.

37

A Burned Bridge

They were so close to Union lines and freedom, but their food was gone and their bodies were ready to give out. Their goal was to reach Brashear City and freedom or die trying.

Flory knew the area and led the way through floodwaters eighteen inches deep as they attempted to stay out of sight. The war had taken its toll on the region. Buildings, homes, and fields were neglected and falling apart, sagging under the strain of four years of war. The men passed silently through this ghostly landscape and by midnight they approached Centreville.[1]

Not a person stirred in the village. Loring and Flory slipped through the town unseen. Reaching the edge of town, Loring's sharp eyes caught the silhouette of a man on his porch. They hid in the shadows until he stepped inside before they continued. They moved close to the Teche River and followed its banks. The upper decks of a Confederate steamer protruding from the water where it had sunk was a sure sign they were ever closer to freedom.

Marching onward, they came near Camp Bissel, a rebel camp in which Flory, under the command of General Banks, had fought the previous year.[2] Flory pointed out the battle site as they moved forward. Loring's hamstrings contracted again. Hunched over, he suffered horribly as he waddled along, trying to keep up as they pushed on toward Brashear City. Flory was weak, feverish, and exhausted. He helped his friend as best he could but it was all he could do to remain upright himself.

Flory stumbled and fell, scraping the side of his head. Loring offered encouragement and helped Flory up. The sun rose and the men fell into a thicket to rest for a couple of hours. Nearly completely exhausted, they walked another mile and then made camp in a cane field for the remainder of the day. They made a very small fire and each ate their last handful of parched corn, scraped from the bottoms of their knapsacks, and hoped no one would see the few wisps of smoke from the fire. They were so worn out that not a word was spoken. Loring looked at Flory. If it were not for the fact that they were traveling together, he would not recognize him. Loring wondered if he was as unrecognizable; would his family recognize him when he was finally reunited with them?[3] They slept the rest of the day.

Waking up, Loring commented to Flory that this would be the twenty-fifth night of their escape. Just sixteen miles to freedom. The date was December 7, and around 3:00 p.m. Loring stood up. He reached down and helped Flory to his feet. They moved to the edge of the cane field. Finding a deer trail, they followed it around the town, staying low and crawling through the thickets and brambles when necessary. They stopped and waited for what seemed an eternity for night to fall.

When it was completely dark they began to creep forward. Flory was in the lead. He knew a shortcut to Berwick's Bay that would eliminate fully three miles from their march, but it would take them through some of the most difficult growth the area had to offer. The shortcut road was completely overgrown but it seemed the best option. The men used what little strength they had left to pull themselves through the cane, bamboo, and brush. They finally emerged at a juncture with the main road, saving three miles around the swamp, just as Flory had recalled.

Loring surveyed the road. The ravages of war were evident, with telegraph poles strewn across it. There was no one in sight. Loring turned to give Flory the okay but found his comrade had collapsed in a heap. Loring waddled back to Flory's side. Flory looked up and told Loring, "I can go no further; leave me here." Loring was quick to respond. "It is not in accordance with the stipulations."[4] "In just a few hours we will be within Union lines. We have come too far to give up now." Flory dug deep and with Loring's help gained his feet. The men leaned against each other. They dragged themselves down the road toward a train trestle spanning three hundred feet across a bayou. The only problem was the trestle lay in ruins. It had been burned and only its pilings protruded above the water line every fifteen feet. Flory was stunned and sank to the ground; he did not recall this bridge.

A Burned Bridge

Loring considered their options. They could find a way across, or they could turn back, crawl through the dense undergrowth, and skirt around the swamp, which would add another eight miles to their trek. They had to find a way across.

Ever resourceful, Loring devised a plan to shimmy across on a board placed on top of the pilings.[5] Once across, they would pull up the board behind them and place it on top of the next two pilings, until they were entirely across. Both men searched for a board long and sturdy enough to span the fifteen-foot intervals. They found none. Frustrated, Flory told Loring they would have to backtrack. Loring perked up. Yes! Backtrack to the telegraph poles lying on the road. They were certainly long enough. It would, however, require both men to walk a half mile back to retrieve a pole and then carry it back. Flory looked up at Loring: "I am not sure I have the strength." Both men walked, crawled, and dragged themselves the half mile back to the telegraph poles. Reaching the poles, it took them thirty minutes to find one long enough and that they could actually pick up. Straining to lift it between them, they dragged, pushed, rolled, and kicked it the half mile back to the burned trestle.

A rumble of thunder could be heard as they stood on the bank peering at the pilings across the bayou. This was going to be more difficult than they first imagined. It was difficult to see. The moon was only a sliver in the sky and the clouds were quickly rolling in. With a push they secured the pole across the first set of pilings. Loring straddled the pole and pushed himself across. On the next piling he held tight as Flory did the same. The pole was twice the required length, which helped to counterbalance it, making it more stable.

Slowly they pushed the pole along. Sometimes they hit their mark. Other times they had to pull it back and try again. This was done while both men balanced themselves on top of a piling not more than four feet around. As they reached the middle of the bayou the approaching storm hit with its full fury. The wind blew the rain sideways and the temperature dropped below freezing. The telegraph pole became slippery and several times each man nearly fell the thirty feet into the depths below. With tremendous focus and determination, they reached the opposite shore. The rain beat down upon the men. Flory looked to the heavens, saying, "With your almighty guidance we have made it." With adrenaline coursing through their veins they screamed in jubilation, competing with the claps of thunder.

Flory suddenly brought the celebration to a halt. He grabbed Loring by the arm. He remembered that there was another trestle crossing less than a mile farther down the road. Loring turned and looked at his friend. "Do you mean to say there is another bridge and it may also be destroyed? Come, now, can any of this be worse than Camp Groce?" Together they turned into the teeth of the storm and pushed on.

38

Chimneys on the Horizon

Both men knew they would most likely find the next bridge in a similar state of destruction. But they were too exhausted and weak to carry the telegraph pole a mile to find out. They would have to take their chances. The road was overgrown with cane and underbrush and they had to lean forward, using their weight to push their way through. An hour of fighting their way through the tangled mess left them on the bank of another bayou. They stared across the open expanse where the bridge used to be. A few pilings stood in the water, marking the way to freedom.

The rain had slowed to a steady drizzle but the wind whipped the cold, wet men. Flory sank to the ground. Some movement on the opposite bank caught Loring's eye. It was difficult to tell what it was. Could it be a Union army tent?[1] Was there a Union sentry posted near the former bridge? Was the entire Union army, freedom, and home just beyond the bayou? Loring pointed and yelled over the wind to Flory. He could barely make out what seemed to be a line of chimneys. These must be houses filled with Federal soldiers. Loring yelled so that the sentry might come to their aid, but the wind was blowing toward the men and they could not be heard. Loring looked down at Flory. They would have to backtrack nearly a mile to retrieve the pole in order to cross the bayou. Flory screamed with frustration. "How can this be? What else must we endure? We are so close!" Loring turned and hobbled back toward the telegraph poles. Flory crawled after him.

Back through the brush they stumbled. They found the pole but then discovered a plank that was lighter than the telegraph pole; it would work better. Barely able to pick it up, they shouldered it and slogged back to the bayou. Reaching the final obstacle, they positioned the plank and pushed it out onto the first piling. Loring crawled across with Flory following. Fifteen feet at a time, they inched closer to freedom. The men hugged the plank and pulled themselves across. The wind whipped the rain sideways, making it difficult to see. Inch by inch, foot by foot, Loring and Flory crawled across the bayou pilings. Reaching the final piling, they pushed the plank out as far as it would go. It didn't reach. It was too short! They were mere feet from shore and freedom but could not reach it. Perched twenty feet above the water, the men sat and shivered silently as they stared out into the darkness.

Loring stood up, nearly falling off the piling. "Colonel, did you hear that?" The wind had suddenly carried upon it a very distinct sound, a sound that Loring had heard thousands of times before: the sound of a bell.[2] Flory looked up at Loring. Loring strained to listen. He looked Flory square in the eye. "I heard a bell. I heard a bell! That bell bears a message from home. That is the bell of a Union gunboat! Four strokes—it is ten o'clock. Those aren't chimneys in the distance, they are smokestacks from Union gunboats!"

Flory's eyes widened as Loring's words penetrated the exhaustion and pain of their current situation. This was the encouragement the men needed. Loring pushed the plank down at an angle into the water. He pulled out the few remaining scraps of the enameled cloth and Flory pulled off his serape; they tied them together and secured one end to the piling. They descended into the cold, dark waters. They would swim the final fifty feet to shore. Loring helped lower Flory down the plank and then followed close behind as Flory sank into the cold blackness. Barely able to keep their heads above water, they thrashed and clawed their way across. A loose telegraph wire hung close to the water. Grabbing it, they pulled themselves the final twenty feet to the bank and then up onto dry land. The last ditch had been forded.

Leaning against each other, the men marched toward the army tent. Shivering nearly uncontrollably, they approached the tent, only to find it was merely scraps of cloth blowing in the wind. They turned directly into the wind and marched toward the smokestacks of the gunboats in the distance. The sound of a ship's bell beckoned them home. Flory knew that army troops would not expect anybody to be walking up on them from this direction with the bridge being out. To alert any unsuspecting troops of their approach both men shouted "Hurrah!" as a warning every ten steps.

Chimneys on the Horizon

The sound of waves breaking on shore and the smell of the sea reached the men. The vague lines of Union ships became distinct in the distance. Overcome with emotion, Loring and Flory walked to the edge of the beach and stood in the salty waters. "Colonel, it is finished; and we are free!" Loring hailed the closest ship. "Ship Ahoy! Please send a boat quick for two Union Officers who are starving and freezing."[3] There was no response. Unable to wait, they had to seek shelter or freeze to death. Flory suggested that they go to the nearby fort and seek refuge there.

Cautiously they moved on, concerned that their own soldiers could mistake them for Confederates. A short distance from the bay they encountered three houses. Loring pounded on the door of the first one they came to, waking somebody inside. The owner, an Irishman, cautiously called out, "Who's there?" Loring replied, "Two soldiers wet to the skin from the storm. We want food and fire. Are you alone?" Afraid, the owner asked if they were Yankees or Confederates. Loring demanded that they be let in. The Irishman explained that if he let them in his house would be burned and he could be hanged. Captain Bailey Vincent and his Partisan Rangers near Pattersonville would see to that if they found out.[4] Loring and Flory had come too far to freeze to death on the doorstep of freedom.

As persuasively as possible, Loring told the Irishman that they were Yankees and could pay for the night. The hinges of the door squeaked as it slowly opened to allow the men entrance to the house. In a commanding tone Loring told the Irishman to make a fire as quickly as possible. Loring shuffled across the room and leaned against the fireplace mantle. His hamstrings were so contracted he was unable to sit.

39

Lincoln Coffee and a Civilized Bed

The Irishman understood clearly from Loring's tone that he was not to be trifled with. With no wood in the house, the Irishman rushed outside and tore several pieces of fencing down from his yard enclosure. He ran back in and used them to make a fire. As the fire crackled Loring insisted that the Irishman bring whatever food he had available and put it on the table. He and Flory would cook it so the Irishman could go back to sleep. All the Irishman had to offer was some cornmeal, but he made up for it with some real coffee; Lincoln coffee![1]

Flory cooked up the cornmeal as Loring boiled the coffee. Both men stripped off their wet clothes, hung them by the fire, and wrapped themselves in blankets the Irishman provided. Flory was in bad shape; he could no longer stand and crawled closer to the fire. With his belly full of hot coffee and cornmeal he curled up on the floor next to the fire and was soon sleeping. Loring was unable to stretch out. His contracted hamstrings prevented him from fully sitting so he propped himself up in the corner near the fire. Here he stood watch, listening to the raging storm outside. Suffering but ever vigilant, he was happy to be inside Union lines. Throughout the night he recalled the escape and the obstacles and challenges he and Flory had overcome. A ship's bell could be heard on the wind. Eight bells; it was 4:00 a.m. on December 8, twenty-five days after their escape from Camp Groce.[2]

Flory shook Loring. "Lieutenant, are you up?" Flory looked out a window and could see a small boat rowing toward shore. It had to be the boat that Loring had hailed the night before. They gathered their belongings and left a greenback that they had saved for just such an occasion. Nearly falling out the door in their excitement, they leaned against each other and shuffled down to the beach and the waiting boat. Loring stepped toward the officer in charge, saluted, and introduced himself and Flory. The officer's mouth hung open as he stared at the filthy, ragged men. Loring and Flory both provided information that only a Union officer would know in an attempt to convince the officer in charge that they were who they claimed to be.[3] Finally convinced, the officer in charge barked some orders. Loring and Flory were helped aboard a small boat and rowed out to the USS *Carrabasset*, the same tin-clad gunboat Loring had commanded on his way to New Orleans nine months previously, now anchored in Berwick's Bay.

Safely onboard, Loring and Flory were given some much needed attention, beginning with a bath! For the first time in months they bathed with actual soap. It took an hour of scrubbing to scrape several layers of grime, crud, and dirt from the creases of their bodies. Sporting a new set of clothes, Loring looked in a mirror and said, "Ah, there you are." With new clothes, a bed with clean linens, and good, warm food, the men reveled in the paradise they had dreamed of for more than eight months. Flory went up on deck. Loring folded his raggedy clothes. He put these aside, along with the scraps of boots, moccasins, patched socks, penknife, Mrs. Coffin's withered rose leaves, the forged gate pass, and traveling orders as mementoes of the long trek home, and joined Flory on deck.[4]

40

The Surprise

That evening over dinner Loring and Flory told their tale to all those who would listen. The next morning, after enjoying a night in a bed with clean linens for the first time in eight months, they were rowed ashore. They boarded a train in Brashear City and made their way to New Orleans eighty miles away. The cane fields, swamps, and bayous of the countryside seemed surreal as they skipped along the rails. Loring and Flory stepped off the train and into the station in New Orleans.

Not more than fifty feet away, inside the doors of the station, Loring noticed a man crying while hugging and embracing several children and a woman. It was clear that this was some sort of family reunion with a loved one. As Loring continued closer he saw the man's face. It seemed familiar. There was also something familiar about the man's voice. Loring stopped. Flory looked at him and asked if everything was okay. Loring pointed at the man and rubbed his eyes in disbelief. It couldn't be. "This man is back from the dead."

Loring approached the man, took him by the arm, and asked, "Duncan?[1] Duncan Smith from Calcasieu Pass, is that you?" This was the same man and his family for whom Loring had been ordered to provide safe passage aboard the USS *Wave*. The same man who had jumped overboard when the Confederates captured the *Wave* and the same man who swam to shore but was reported murdered by Loring's captors. It was indeed Mr. Smith. Smith did not say a word but stared at Loring. Loring spoke, "Don't you recognize me?" Loring was a skeleton of his former self but the voice was familiar to Smith. Slowly recognition crept over Smith until finally he realized this was Lieutenant Loring, the man who had tried to bring him and his family safely to New Orleans.

The excitement of being reunited with his family and now with the man who had tried to save them all was overwhelming. Loring asked Smith what had happened to him. Smith explained that after swimming to shore he lay in hiding for five months and eventually made his way to New Orleans. After arriving he worked to secure passage for his family. They had just arrived on the same train as Loring and Flory. It was all too much to comprehend. Smith thanked Loring for all that he had tried to do for them. Loring wished him well, rejoined Flory, and continued on out of the train station. The two men parted ways and reported to their respective headquarters. That evening the men enjoyed dinner together and reminisced about their adventure and remembered their comrades. The following day they parted company for good. There were no words exchanged between the men. A simple, knowing handshake was all that was needed. Flory was sent home to Indiana and Loring was ordered to the Washington Navy Yard to recuperate.

41

Washington Navy Yard

Loring arrived in Washington in mid-December and reported to the Navy Yard. He presented his orders from Commodore Palmer dated December 9, 1864, which acknowledged his escape and sent him north.[1] His health prevented him from returning to active field duty immediately. He was placed on waiting orders and told to remain in Washington. The transition to regular military duty was not easy. Loring had spent the previous eight months scrounging for food, tending to his men, strategizing about escape, and simply trying to survive. The sudden change at times caught him off guard, with the ample food causing the most serious issue.

Loring was still so hungry all the time he had difficulty keeping a meal down. He was not used to the quality or the quantity of food available after the starvation rations in the prison and on the road. He quickly discovered that it was better for his constitution to eat several small meals throughout the day rather than a couple of large ones. His hamstrings still caused him issues and would contract, causing him to be bent over and shuffle when he tried to walk more than a couple hundred yards at one time. But the physician who examined him explained that would subside in the coming weeks. The same physician, however, was very concerned about the condition of Loring's feet. They would require some attention and constant care to avoid further spread of infection and possible amputation. The doctor had never seen such terrible blisters and warned Loring there would definitely be some permanent scarring. Loring told the doctor it was a small price to pay to be free once again.

By the end of December Loring had put some weight back on his depleted frame. While his blisters had begun to heal, the cold winter temperatures often left him with very cold and numb feet. He wore his boots a size larger than previously to accommodate thick wool socks, which not only helped to keep his feet warm but seemed to provide some cushioning as well. Winter wore on, and Loring found that after just a few weeks he was able to make himself useful. Approaching his commanding officer, he inquired about a position where he could be assigned some duty and actually contribute to the war effort. On January 20, 1865, he received orders from Secretary of the Navy Gideon Welles to report for duty on board the receiving ship USS *North Carolina* in New York harbor. Arriving in New York on February 3, Loring collected his $95.60 for mileage and reported for duty.[2]

Loring regained his old strength quickly but was hampered by his feet. Never one to be sickly, he reveled in his newfound vigor. It was only now that he began to fully realize just how bad off he had actually been while in prison and on the run. He did not dwell on that and was glad to be useful again. He immersed himself in his duties as quartermaster and receiving clerk.

He was bothered, however. Just days after his escape and arrival in Washington it had come to his attention that the battle of Calcasieu had been viewed as a disaster and his surrender of the *Wave* was an embarrassment. All that time while rotting in Camp Groce Loring had taken solace in the fact that he had done everything possible to prepare for a fight on the Calcasieu while still fulfilling his orders. Yet come to find out his name had been dragged through the mud for the surrender of the *Wave* shortly after the battle. Admiral Farragut himself expressed his displeasure, saying, "They say that each vessel made a most gallant defense, but finally had to surrender, having so many killed or wounded, while the letters show that there were only 10 wounded aboard the Granite City, two of whom have since died, and 8 wounded on board the Wave, all flesh wounds. This was the desperate fighting that caused them to surrender. The enemy was on shore without cover of any kind. It is mortifying to see my vessels behave so badly, but I have none else but these volunteer officers to send in them."[3] Loring could not let this stand and had to defend his actions and his honor. He drafted a detailed but concise report on the action that occurred at Calcasieu Pass, explaining the situation and circumstances with supporting documentation and orders. His report was received by Secretary Welles on February 28.[4] Loring waited for a response.

Loring soon received orders to return to duty in the Washington Navy Yards. By April 12, 1865, he was commanding the Naval Rendezvous Office.[5] He would take the opportunity to explain in detail his actions and clear his good name.

Late at night, lying in bed and trying to sleep, Loring would play the events of the battle over and over in his head. It was especially disconcerting that Admiral Farragut thought that Loring could have done more and that Farragut did not think he had put up a good fight. That was absurd. Of all the battles and actions during the course of the war it was this that haunted Loring. He was sure that his potential naval career would be stymied by this.

The weather warmed and the spring of 1865 seemed promising. Lincoln had been reelected president and given his second inaugural speech. General Grant had broken through the lines at Richmond and Lee had just surrendered at a small crossroads in Virginia called Appomattox Court House. The whole war seemed to be ending. Loring and the country were in a good mood. Hearing that President Lincoln and General Grant would be celebrating by attending the theater, Loring purchased a ticket. What better way to celebrate the glorious news of Lee's surrender than to personally cast his eyes upon two of the men he most greatly admired, Lincoln and Grant. Excited, he clutched his ticket admitting him to the orchestra level at Ford's Theatre to see the play *Our American Cousin.* Loring looked forward to an enjoyable and memorable evening.

42

I Held Lincoln

Loring limped through the streets of Washington as he made his way to Ford's Theatre the evening of April 14, 1865.[1] He was excited and wanted to arrive early enough so that he could find a good seat. Inside Loring was surprised to see that so many people had already arrived. He surveyed the theater and tried out a couple of seats in the orchestra level until he found one that provided an unobstructed view of the private box where General Grant and the president would be seated. Anxious about the prospect of seeing both men, he chatted with those around him. The conversation among the evening's patrons focused on the recent surrender of General Lee, the prospects of the war ending, and the special guests that they all hoped would soon arrive. Loring glanced up at the private box reserved for President Lincoln and thought it looked very patriotic. It was festooned with a red, white, and blue bunting, an American flag, and a portrait of President Washington. The orchestra began to play, and the audience took their seats and settled in. Loring glanced up at the private box again but did not see either of the distinguished guests. The curtain opened and the play began.

Loring laughed and enjoyed himself along with the other members of the audience. Losing track of time, he pulled out his recently purchased gold watch. It was 8:32 p.m. The orchestra struck up "Hail to the Chief." Loring turned and looked up to see President and Mrs. Lincoln entering the private box. They were accompanied by another couple whom he did not recognize. Loring stood along with the rest of the audience and applauded the commander in chief. The president nodded, acknowledging the generous outpouring from those in attendance, and then settled into a rocking chair. Loring sat back down and could barely keep his attention focused on stage; he found himself staring at the president every couple of minutes. But the play was engaging, and Loring's attention soon returned to the stage. Loring slapped his thigh as the character Asa Trenchard, played by the actor Harry Hawke, delivered an uproarious soliloquy. As Loring laughed he turned to the woman seated next to him, smiled, and nodded.

Loring stiffened as the unmistakable crack of a gun went off close by. His head snapped toward the sound. He was looking directly at the private box. He watched as a man jumped from the box to the stage floor and heard him yell something before limping off toward the back of the theater. He thought to himself, "This is a strange turn of events for a comedy." A scream from the private box focused Loring's attention. He realized that something was very wrong and could see that the president was slumped in his chair. Mrs. Lincoln was screaming for help. Loring bolted from his seat. His uniform hat fell off his lap as he rushed forward and leapt onto the stage.[2] Adrenaline coursed through his body. The audience erupted and crowded the aisles. Some moved toward the exits as they slowly realized that someone had just injured the president. Loring sprinted to the base of the private box and motioned to two other men to help boost him up. Clawing his way up, he shimmied into the box and slid over the rail. As he gained his feet he saw an army major slumped on the floor in the corner, covered in blood from a gash on his arm and pointing toward the president.

Loring moved toward Lincoln. Another man, a naval officer from the USS *Primrose* by the name of William Flood, had already reached the unconscious president. Loring looked at the officer and told him they needed to move the president out of the chair. Both men took hold of Lincoln and slid him onto the floor. The president's injury was not obvious. Flood cradled the president's head as Loring ran his hands over the president's jacket and torso. There was no blood. Loring looked at Flood. "Where is he injured?" Lincoln's chest heaved as his breathing labored. Loring reached into his pocket and pulled out his ever-present penknife. He opened the small blade and cut the president's necktie, hoping it would ease his breathing.

The door to the private box burst open; three men fell inside and scrambled to the president's side. Still unable to find a wound, Loring barked orders and yelled for a larger knife. One of the men handed a large folding clasp knife to Loring. He opened the four-inch blade and used it to cut away the president's vest from collar to armhole. Flood held up his hand. The injury, "here it is in the back of his head." "The President has been shot!"[3] More people crowded into the private box, seeking to assist. Miss Keene, an actress, rushed to the front of the private box and called out to those below to bring brandy. Rushing back to the entrance of the box, Miss Keene brought the brandy to the president's side, offering it to be administered to Lincoln. As Loring glanced up Miss Keene held the brandy out but in her heightened state and haste she spilled it down Loring's back. Loring yelled, "Get that woman away from here." Miss Harris, who with her fiancé, Major Rathbone, had accompanied the Lincolns, beckoned for Miss Keene to help her with Mrs. Lincoln. Miss Harris took Miss Keene by the arm and guided her toward Mrs. Lincoln. Nodding her head toward Loring she commented, "Come now, that doctor will help the president." Loring thought to himself, "She must think I am a surgeon."

The president's breathing was shallow and the private box was now full of people. A man pushed his way through the crowd and declared that "a place has been secured for Mr. Lincoln across the street." Loring stood. He grabbed the man's hand and pointed. Loring motioned for three men to help him carry the president. "one at the head, one at the feet and legs and a third clasping hands with myself supported the trunk, the hands slightly separated to divide its weight."[4] Loring yelled at the crowd who pushed closer for a view of the president. "Make way!" The men slowly lifted President Lincoln and cautiously carried him downstairs and across the street to the Peterson House. Inside the house the men gently laid the president upon a bed.

Loring stepped back and looked at the stricken president. It did not seem real. He could not believe what he had just witnessed. He lingered for just a moment, gazing at the careworn face of the man who had saved the Union and who was now battling to cling to life. Loring turned and moved down the crowded hallway. He stepped outside into the cool, damp night air. He pushed his way through the throng of people gathered in the street in front of the Peterson House. Half aloud, he said to himself, "How can this be? The war is nearly over."

Loring played the events over in his mind, the gunshot echoing in his thoughts. Deeply focused, he started walking. Thinking to himself, he considered who could have done such a low thing, why with the war nearly over would someone do such a thing? With the coming of spring there had seemed to be a sense that all of this madness was coming to an end. The country was on the eve of peace and now it seemed to be on the verge of slipping back into chaos. The staccato cadence of Loring's boots on the cobblestones pushed him deeper in thought as he continued to walk, his shadow in the lamplights his only companion.

Loring looked up. He suddenly realized he was standing in front of a building. He had unknowingly walked back to the Washington Navy Yard. He wiped the sticky blood from his hands on a sleeve and the back of his uniform coat and stepped inside the dimly lit headquarters office. The officer on duty looked up from behind his desk, yet unaware of the events that had occurred only minutes before at Ford's Theatre. "Yes, lieutenant, what can I help you with?" Loring stiffened and drew himself up to attention. He looked the lieutenant commander squarely in the eye and announced, "I am Lt. Loring. I have returned, Sir, and report for duty."[5]

Afterword

After the Lincoln assassination Loring continued to command the Naval Rendezvous Office until he was placed on waiting orders October 17, 1865, and was mustered out of the service of the U.S. Navy. Loring had hoped to make the navy a career but his health and damaged reputation had taken their toll. He was commissioned an officer in the Revenue Cutter Service in 1865 and was later promoted, reaching the rank of first lieutenant. His health would thereafter stand in his way of ever being promoted to captain.

After the war he married Nellie Cohoun and had five children, three of whom lived to adulthood. The family settled in Owego, New York, in the early 1870s. He was often contacted by former naval officers and enlisted men asking for a letter of reference and testimony of their service to their country so that they might receive a pension. A hearty letter of thanks in consideration of their service was always forwarded to them. Loring himself never received a pension while he was alive.

In December 1899 a U.S. senator from New York, Thomas Collier Platt, introduced bill S. 281 on the Senate floor to "restore Benjamin W. Loring to the Revenue Cutter Service."[1] On January 11, 1900, the bill was submitted in consideration for Loring's exemplary service record during the Civil War, recommending that he be promoted to captain in the Revenue Cutter Service and to collect pay at that rank while on permanent waiting orders; it was similar to receiving a pension.[2] The bill, with an attached report, was submitted to the Committee on Commerce and was recommended for approval by Lyman J. Gage, secretary of the treasury. The committee approved the bill.[3] On February 6, 1900, the bill was read and passed over without any action.[4] On February 8 Senator Platt asked the Senate to again consider the bill.[5] It was read for a third time and passed. However, on February

12, 1900, the bill was referred back to the Committee on Interstate and Foreign Commerce, where it languished and was never acted upon.[6] Loring died on December 2, 1902, and the matter was forgotten. It is now our duty to see that Loring receives the recognition he is due.

NOTES

1. Getting in the Fight

1. *War of the Rebellion*, ser. 1, vol. 28, part 1 reports, 123.

2. Morgan, *A Little Short of Boats*, 134–40.

3. Loring, personal log, 1.

4. Orders, U.S. secretary of the navy, February 6, 1862, from the collection of Mr. and Mrs. John Loring Hamm (hereafter Hamm Collection).

5. Loring to Lillie Loring, May 16, 1862, Hamm Collection.

6. Letter from rear admiral, July 5, 1863, Hamm Collection.

7. Letter from secretary of the navy, July 13, 1863, Hamm Collection.

8. *War of the Rebellion*, ser. 1, 28:402.

9. Letter from secretary of the navy, October 21, 1863, Hamm Collection.

2. The *Wave*

1. Orders, secretary of the navy, November 18, 1863, Hamm Collection.

2. Letter from Rear Adm. David Porter, March 3, 1864, Hamm Collection.

3. Orders, Rear Admiral Porter, December 2, 1863, Hamm Collection.

4. Letter from Commander Palmer, March 22, 1864, Hamm Collection.

5. Loring, personal log, 3.

6. Loring, personal log, 3.

7. Lisarelli, *Last Prison*, 168. Contains the list of the USS *Wave*'s crew.

8. U.S. Naval History and Heritage Command Center Archives, "Navy Medal of Honor: Civil War 1861–65," https://www.history.navy.mil/browse-by-topic/heritage/awards/decorations/medal-of-honor/civil-war-medal-of-honor-recipients.html.

9. Lisarelli, *Last Prison*, 168.

10. Loring, personal log, 4.

3. A Seasick *Wave*

1. Loring, personal log, 5.

2. Loring, personal log, 7.

3. Loring, personal log, 9.

4. No Coal

1. Loring, personal log, 9.

2. Orders, Commodore James. S. Palmer, May 4, 1864, Hamm Collection.

3. Loring, report to Secretary of the Navy Gideon Welles outlining events at Calcasieu Pass, December 1865, appendix, 393–95, Hamm Collection.

4. Loring report to Welles re: Calcasieu Pass, 393–95, Hamm Collection.

5. Loring, personal log, 10.
6. Loring, personal log, 10.

5. The Enemy Is Close By

1. Loring, personal log, 13.
2. Loring report to Welles re: Calcasieu Pass, 393–95, Hamm Collection.
3. Loring, personal log, 14.
4. Loring, personal log, 14.

6. A Precious Rose

1. Loring, personal log, 17.
2. Loring, personal log, 16.
3. Loring, personal log, 18.
4. Loring, personal log, 18.

7. Chicken Feed

1. Loring, personal log, 20.
2. Loring, personal log, 21.
3. Loring, personal log, 22.

8. Prison

1. Loring, personal log, 23.
2. Loring, personal log, 28.
3. Lisarelli, *Last Prison*, 73.
4. Loring, personal log, 24.

9. Escape!

1. Loring, personal log, 39.
2. Loring, personal log, 40.
3. Loring, personal log, 40.
4. Loring, personal log, 47.
5. Loring, personal log, 49.
6. Loring, personal log, 50–51.
7. Loring, personal log, 51.
8. Loring, personal log, 51.

10. Through the Wall

1. Loring, personal log, 26.
2. Loring, personal log, 57.
3. Loring, personal log, 55.
4. Loring, personal log, 56.
5. Loring, personal log, 57.
6. Loring, personal log, 58.
7. Loring, personal log, 59.

8. Loring, personal log, 58.

9. Loring, personal log, 59.

10. Loring, personal log, 59.

11. Loring, personal log, 60.

12. Loring, personal log, 61.

11. On the Outside

1. Loring, personal log, 62.

2. Loring, personal log, 62.

3. Loring, personal log, 63.

4. Loring, personal log, 64.

5. Loring, personal log, 65.

6. Loring, personal log, 65.

7. Loring, personal log, 64.

8. Loring, personal log, 66.

9. Loring, personal log, 67.

12. Plantations

1. Loring, personal log, 69.

2. Loring, personal log, 70.

3. Loring, personal log, 71.

4. Loring, personal log, 72.

5. Loring, personal log, 73.

6. Loring, personal log, 74.

7. Loring, personal log, 75.

13. Dog Ranch

1. Loring, personal log, 76.

2. Loring, personal log, 77.

3. Loring, personal log, 78.

4. Loring, personal log, 79.

5. Loring, personal log, 80.

6. Loring, personal log, 81.

14. De Doe Is Dead?!

1. Loring, personal log, 82.

2. Loring, personal log, 83.

3. Loring, personal log, 84.

4. Loring, personal log, 85.

5. Loring, personal log, 86.

15. The Hunter

1. Loring, personal log, 87.

2. Loring, personal log, 88.

3. Loring, personal log, 89.

4. Loring, personal log, 90.

5. Loring, personal log, 91.

6. Loring, personal log, 92.

7. Loring, personal log, 92.

8. Loring, personal log, 93.

9. Loring, personal log, 94.

10. Loring, personal log, 94.

11. Loring, personal log, 94.

12. Loring, personal log, 95.

16. Interrogation

1. Loring, personal log, 95.

2. Loring, personal log, 96.

3. Loring, personal log, 95.

4. Loring, personal log, 95.

5. Loring, personal log, 96.

6. Loring, personal log, 97.

17. A Night Drive

1. Loring, personal log, 98.

2. Loring, personal log, 99.

3. Loring, personal log, 99–100.

4. Loring, personal log, 100.

5. Loring, personal log, 100.

18. A Confederate Bastille

1. Loring, personal log, 101.

2. Loring, personal log, 101.

3. Loring, personal log, 102.

19. Anderson Grimes County Jail

1. Loring, personal log, 104.

2. Loring, personal log, 105.

3. Loring, personal log, 106.

4. Loring, personal log, 107.

5. Grimes County Sheriff's Office, "Sheriffs of Grimes County, Texas," http://www.grimescountyso.org/History1.htm.

6. Loring, personal log, 108.

7. Loring, personal log, 109.

8. Loring, personal log, 110.

9. Loring, personal log, 112.

10. Loring, personal log, 115.

20. The Old Pen Again

1. Loring, personal log, 117.
2. Loring, personal log, 118.
3. Loring, personal log, 119.
4. Loring, personal log, 119.
5. Loring, personal log, 120.
6. Loring, personal log, 122.
7. Loring, personal log, 123.
8. Loring, personal log, 124.

21. Deadliest Killer

1. Loring, personal log, 126.
2. Loring, personal log, 127.

22. Making the Best of It

1. Loring, personal log, 129.
2. Loring, personal log, 132.
3. Loring, personal log, 133.
4. Loring, personal log, 134.
5. Loring, personal log, 134.
6. Loring, personal log, 134.
7. Loring, personal log, 135.

23. The Swamp

1. Loring, personal log, 137.
2. Lisarelli, *Last Prison*, 101.
3. Loring, personal log, 139.
4. Loring, personal log, 140.
5. Loring, personal log, 140.
6. Loring, personal log, 141.
7. Loring, personal log, 141.
8. Loring, personal log, 144.
9. Loring, personal log, 145.

24. Tied Up

1. Loring, personal log, 147.
2. Loring, personal log, 147.
3. Loring, personal log, 148.
4. Loring, personal log, 148.
5. Loring, personal log, 148.
6. Loring, personal log, 151.
7. Loring, personal log, 152.
8. Loring, personal log, 153.

9. Loring, personal log, 154.
10. Loring, personal log, 155.
11. Loring, personal log, 156.

25. The Power of the Pen(cil)

1. Loring, personal log, 157.
2. Loring, personal log, 158.
3. Loring, personal log, 158, 159.
4. Loring, personal log, 163.
5. Loring, personal log, 160.
6. Loring, personal log, 162.
7. Loring, personal log, 162.
8. Loring, personal log, 163.
9. Loring, personal log, 163.
10. Loring, personal log, 164.

26. Navigating by the Wind

1. Loring, personal log, 164.
2. Loring, personal log, 166.
3. Loring, personal log, 166.
4. Loring, personal log, 167.
5. Loring, personal log, 167.
6. Loring, personal log, 168.
7. Loring, personal log, 169.
8. Loring, personal log, 170.

27. Parched Corn

1. Loring, personal log, 173.
2. Loring, personal log, 174.
3. Loring, personal log, 175.
4. Loring, personal log, 178.

28. Over the River and through the Woods

1. Loring, personal log, 181.
2. Loring, personal log, 183.

29. Bear Swamp

1. Loring, personal log, 186.
2. Loring, personal log, 188.
3. Loring, personal log, 189.

30. Confederate Potatoes

1. Loring, personal log, 192.
2. Loring, personal log, 193.

3. Loring, personal log, 193.

4. Loring, personal log, 194.

5. Loring, personal log, 196.

6. Loring, personal log, 197.

7. Loring, personal log, 197.

8. Loring, personal log, 198.

31. Goodbye, Texas

1. Loring, personal log, 202.

2. Loring, personal log, 202.

32. Home Guard and Yankee Prisoners

1. Loring, personal log, 204, 205.

2. Loring, personal log, 206.

3. Loring, personal log, 208.

4. Loring, personal log, 209.

5. Loring, personal log, 209.

33. Old Friends?

1. Loring, personal log, 211.

2. Loring, personal log, 211.

3. Loring, personal log, 212.

4. Loring, personal log, 213.

5. Loring, personal log, 214.

34. Your Passes or Your Life!

1. Loring, personal log, 217.

2. Loring, personal log, 218.

3. Loring, personal log, 218.

4. Loring, personal log, 219.

5. Loring, personal log, 220.

6. Loring, personal log, 221.

7. The entire exchange with Colonel Brough is taken from Loring, personal log, 222–24.

8. Loring, personal log, 225.

9. Loring, personal log, 226.

35. Where Is My Penknife?

1. Loring, personal log, 227.

2. Loring, personal log, 228.

3. Loring, personal log, 229.

4. Loring, personal log, 229.

5. Loring, personal log, 231.

6. Loring, personal log, 232.

7. Loring, personal log, 234.

8. Loring, personal log, 235.

9. Loring, personal log, 235.

36. The Last Toenail

1. Loring, personal log, 238.

2. Loring, personal log, 239.

3. Loring, personal log, 240.

4. Loring, personal log, 241.

5. Loring, personal log, 243.

37. A Burned Bridge

1. Loring, personal log, 245.

2. Loring, personal log, 246.

3. Loring, personal log, 247.

4. Loring, personal log, 249.

5. Loring, personal log, 250.

38. Chimneys on the Horizon

1. Loring, personal log, 254.

2. Loring, personal log, 255.

3. Loring, personal log, 258.

4. Loring, personal log, 259–60.

39. Lincoln Coffee and a Civilized Bed

1. Loring, personal log, 261.

2. Loring, personal log, 263.

3. Loring, personal log, 264.

4. Loring, personal log, 265.

40. The Surprise

1. Loring, personal log, 266.

41. Washington Navy Yard

1. Commodore Palmer, U.S. Naval HQ, New Orleans, to Lieutenant Loring, December 9, 1864, Hamm Collection.

2. Orders, Secretary of the Navy Gideon Welles, January 20, 1865, Hamm Collection.

3. Report No. 199, Rear Admiral Farragut, in U.S. Naval War Records Office, *Official Records*, ser. 1, 21:249–50.

4. Loring report to Welles re: Calcasieu Pass, 393–98, Hamm Collection.

5. A. Smith, chief, Bureau of Equipment and Recruiting, to Loring, April 12, 1865, Hamm Collection.

42. I Held Lincoln

1. Loring, personal log, 232.
2. Loring, personal log, 232–33.
3. Loring, personal log, 232–33.
4. Loring, personal log, 232–33.
5. Loring, personal log, 268.

Afterword

1. U.S. Senate, 56th Congress, 1st sess., *Congressional Record* 33, pt. 1, 90.
2. Report No. 58, January 11, 1900, U.S. Senate, 56th Congress, 1st sess. (synopsis of Loring's service record, including details of his assisting President Lincoln at Ford's Theatre, April 14, 1865).
3. Report No. 58, January 11, 1900, U.S. Senate, 56th Congress, 1st sess.
4. U.S. Senate, 56th Congress, 1st sess., *Congressional Record* 33, pt. 2, 1561.
5. U.S. Senate, 56th Congress, 1st sess., *Congressional Record* 33, pt. 2, 1650.
6. U.S. Senate, 56th Congress, 1st sess., *Congressional Record* 33, pt. 2, 1727.

BIBLIOGRAPHY

Unpublished Sources

Loring, Lt. Benjamin W. Personal log detailing the events of 1864. Mr. and Mrs. John Loring Hamm Collection.

—————. Personal papers, including Loring's prison diary, escape diary, escape map, forged passes, letters to his sister Lillie, and letters from navy officers. Mr. and Mrs. John Loring Hamm Collection.

U.S. Navy. Original navy orders of Lt. Benjamin W. Loring, USN. Mr. and Mrs. John Loring Hamm Collection.

Published Sources

Lisarelli, Danial Francis. *The Last Prison: The Untold Story of Camp Groce CSA.* Privately published, 1999.

Morgan, James A., III. *A Little Short of Boats: The Battles of Ball's Bluff and Edwards Ferry, October 21–22, 1861.* Rev. ed. New York: Savas Beatie, 2011.

U.S. Naval War Records Office. *Official Records of the Union and Confederate Navies in the War of the Rebellion.* 30 vols. Washington DC: Government Printing Office, 1894–1922.

U.S. Senate. Report No. 58. 56th Congress, 1st sess., January 11, 1900.

The War of the Rebellion: A Compilation of the Official Records of the Union and Confederate Armies. 70 vols. Washington DC: Government Printing Office, 1881–1901.